THE NATIVITY
By Arnoul Greban

Translated by Shelley Sewall

Southern Illinois University Press

Carbondale and Edwardsville

Printed in the United States of America
Edited by Susan Thornton
Designed by Edward King
Production supervised by Hillside Studio

Library of Congress Cataloging-in-Publication Data
Greban, Arnoul, ca. 1420–1471.
    [Le Mystère de la nativité de Nostre Saulveur Jhesu Crist. English]
    The Nativity / by Arnoul Greban: translated by Shelley Sewall.
       p.   cm.
    Translation of: Le Mystère de la nativité de Nostre Saulveur Jhesu
Crist.
    "An edited literal translation in prose"—Pref.
    1. Jesus Christ—Nativity—Drama.   I. Sewall, Shelley, 1937–
II. Title.
    PQ1357.N2G7413   1991
842'.2—dc20   90-33187
ISBN 0-8093-1646-3   CIP

CONTENTS

PREFACE

The Nativity by Arnoul Greban is a fifteenth-century French Christmas play based on an orthodox interpretation of the Gospels of Matthew and Luke. It is part of Greban's vast cyclic drama in verse, *The Mystery of the Passion* (c. 1450), which was performed over a period of several days on the French medieval polyscenic stage.

When I extracted *The Nativity* from *The Mystery of the Passion*, I took about five thousand lines of verse (lines 3333 to 8019) from the thirty-five-thousand-line drama and assigned to those lines the traditional titles: *The Nativity of Our Lord* and *The Play of the Three Kings*. I added scene divisions and titles for clarity. This is an edited literal translation in prose; songs retain stanzas and refrains. Greban's syntax is largely preserved with modernization of punctuation. He slips in many quotations from the Bible, translated here in the King James Version, that blend smoothly with the dramatic text. Anachronisms typical of French medieval mysteries are retained.

This translation should increase rapport between the disciplines of French medieval studies, which emphasizes literary analysis, and theater history, which concerns the conjectural reconstruction of staging based on analysis of stage directions, stage plans, and iconographic evidence. My mentor is a great scholar of French medieval literature, D. D. R. Owen of the University of St. Andrews, whose definitive translations are my inspiration. Robert Sarlós and Edward Langhans, disciples of the theater historian A. M. Nagler, showed me sound methods of investigating medieval evidence. Sarlós's suggestions for revisions were invaluable. I also wish to thank Richard Davis, theater historian, for advice concerning the Introduction; Robert Page, director, for teaching me to direct large-scale productions; Manfred Kusch and Marc Blanchard, professors of French literature, for their interest in my work; my daughters, the actresses Charlotte London and Lia London, for their belief in my unicorn mission; and Robert Phillips, the editor, for assistance with format.

The midfifteenth-century Arras miniatures are from Manuscript 625 of the Bibliothèque d'Arras, which contains three hundred fifty miniatures illustrating two dramatic texts attributed to Eustache Mercadé: *The Mystery of the Passion* and *The Vengeance of Our Lord.* The Arras miniatures are on pages 20, 30, 52, 61, and 74, and are used with kind permission of the Bibliothèque d'Arras. The midsixteenth-century Valenciennes miniatures are from Manuscript fr 12536 and Manuscript Rot-I-7-3 of the Bibliothèque Nationale; they show the stage and staging of the Valenciennes version of *The Mystery of the Passion* in 1547. The Valenciennes miniatures are on pages x–xi, 22, 25, 70, 84, 95, and 103, and are used with kind permission of the Bibliothèque Nationale.

The Nativity

The fourth day of the Valenciennes Mystery of the Passion

Anthipater

Calcor

Herode

INTRODUCTION

Nativity Texts

Extant Nativity texts for the French medieval religious stage date from the thirteenth century; I will trace the development of Nativity texts from liturgical to community drama before turning to Arnoul Greban's text of the midfifteenth century, *The Nativity*. Four extant texts were written prior to Greban's work: the Chantilly manuscripts; the Saint Genevieve collection of four mysteries, including *The Nativity of Our Lord* and *The Play of the Three Kings*; the Burgundian *Passion of Semur*; and *The Mystery of the Passion* by Eustache Mercadé.[1]

The Chantilly *Nativity*, a play of five hundred lines, is based on a thirteenth-century play that was updated and recopied in the late fifteenth century by nuns. It contains few characters and appears to have been composed for production in a convent.[2] The characters quote the Gospels, liturgy, and earlier Latin dramas, sometimes in Latin. There is also a fragment of three hundred lines of another *Nativity* that contains only scenes at the Temple and at Herod's palace.

The Saint Genevieve collection of four mysteries is significant because it was in the repertory of the Confrérie de la Passion. Although the original version of these texts dates from the midfourteenth century, there is no evidence that the Confrérie performed them, in Paris and in the suburbs, before 1398–1402.[3] *The Nativity of Our Lord* is a play of two thousand lines with a combination of liturgical and folk materials; it represents an early

---

1. The Chantilly manuscripts are in Gustave Cohen, ed., *Mystères et moralités du manuscrit 617 de Chantilly* (Geneva: Slatkine Reprints, 1975). The Saint Genevieve collection is in Achille Jubinal, ed., *Mystères inédits du quinzième siècle* (Paris: Téchener, 1837). The Burgundian *Passion de Semur* is in Émile Roy, ed., *Le Mystère de la Passion en France du XIVe au XVIe siècle* (Dijon: Université de Dijon, 1903), *Revue Bourguignonne*, vol. 13. The Mercadé *Passion* is in Jules-Marie Richard, ed., *Le Mystère de la Passion* (Arras: Imprimerie de la Société du Pas-de-Calais, 1891).

2. Cohen, *Mystères*, p. cxxi.

3. Grace Frank, *The Medieval French Drama* (Oxford: Clarendon Press, 1954), pp. 146–47; see also L. Petit de Julleville, *Les Mystères* (Paris: Librairie Hachette, 1880), vol. 1, p. 420.

attempt to develop a cyclic drama when combined with three other plays: *The Play of the Three Kings, The Passion of Our Lord,* and *The Resurrection of Our Lord.*

The Burgundian *Passion of Semur,* dating from the first third of the fifteenth century, is a transitional text between the Saint Genevieve collection and the cyclic dramas of the fifteenth century. This mystery of 9,500 lines contains a *Creation* and a *Nativity* on the first day, and a *Passion* and a *Resurrection* on the second day. The *Nativity* is a provincial play of 1,350 lines for a large cast, featuring a bawdy clown named Rusticus and a debate between female allegorical characters, Sancta Ecclesia and Sinaguogua.

The Mystery of the Passion by Mercadé, dating from the first decade of the fifteenth century, is the first great cyclic drama; this text of twenty-five thousand lines requires four days for its performance. Mercadé's *Nativity* is a placid text for a small cast, including midwives to assist Mary and mischievous shepherds. However, his *Play of the Three Kings* is violent, with vivid scenes of Herod's raging, the Massacre of the Innocents, and Herod's suicide. Mercadé's *Passion* is important because Greban had a copy on hand while he was writing his own version.[4]

Mercadé introduces the Trial in Paradise to give structural unity to his cycle; Greban borrows this structure in his version. The Trial in Paradise is based on Psalm 85:10: "Mercy and truth are met together; righteousness and peace have kissed each other." Mercadé places onstage allegorical characters called the Daughters of God: Mercy, Justice, Truth, Wisdom, and Charity. Greban later adds Peace and subtracts Charity. These characters debate whether mankind should be redeemed after the Fall. In both dramas, Mercy is mankind's most fervent advocate, whereas Justice insists that, like the fallen angels, mankind merits eternal damnation. God decides in favor of humanity, but he is saddened to hear Justice insist that mankind may only be redeemed by the sacrifice of his Son. The playwrights, both clerics, use this allegorical trial to explain why God permits his Son to suffer the Crucifixion. The purpose of Christ's life is presented as a predestined sacrifice that greatly benefits mankind, so it must be patiently endured by Christ, by God the Father and the angels, and by the faithful on earth and in Limbo. The audience may blame Justice for her harshness, while appreciating God's love for mankind and for his Son. The *Creation* is added by Greban, not by Mercadé, to show the Fall before the Redemption.

4. Frank, *Medieval French Drama,* pp. 184–85.

The two greatest writers of mysteries, Arnoul Greban and Jehan
Michel, each composed a cyclic drama entitled *The Mystery of the Passion*.
Greban's text of thirty-five thousand lines was first performed in Paris
around 1450.[5] It is based on religious sources and contains few rubrics
(stage directions). Michel's text of thirty thousand lines was first performed in Angers in 1486. He borrows many lines from Greban, includes
legendary sources, and adds many rubrics. Greban's immense mystery begins with the *Creation* and ends with the *Resurrection*. Michel's work does not
contain a *Nativity* because it includes only the *Ministry* and the *Passion*; his
Resurrection of Our Lord is a separate drama. Greban seems warm, pious, and
compassionate, whereas Michel seems cynical, secular, and sensational.
Michel was a doctor with a gift for dissecting the flaws in human character;
Greban showed more restraint in the selection and treatment of dramatic
material.

The longest Nativity drama, with a huge cast and elaborate rubrics, was
performed in Rouen in 1474. It features shepherds as clowns and lacks the
spirituality of Greban's version.[6]

The texts of mysteries were largely ignored from 1548, when Parliament
piously halted their production, until the nineteenth century, when scholars
rediscovered the plays and began patiently to collate and publish them.
These editors praised the earliest native texts in the vernacular:

> We find a great charm in the mysteries, and we are persuaded that those
> who read them assiduously will be of our opinion. Without speaking of
> the resources offered to the poet by the greatness of the subject matter,
> the expansiveness of the scene, the variety of the tableaux, and the num-
> ber of characters, we find rare qualities in our ancient drama. . . . The
> heroes of mysteries think and act like us. God and the saints have their
> passions just like men.[7]

Despite an impressive list of publications in the nineteenth and twentieth

5. The Greban *Passion* is in Gaston Paris and Gaston Raynaud, eds., *Le Mystère de la Passion d'Arnoul Greban* (Paris: F. Vieweg, Libraire-Éditeur, 1878). The dating of Greban's version
is on p. vii. See also Omer Jodogne, ed., *Le Mystère de la Passion d'Arnoul Greban* (Brussels: Académie royale de Belgique, 1965–83). The Michel *Passion* is in Omer Jodogne, ed., *Le Mystère de
la Passion* (Gembloux: Éditions J. Duculot, 1959).

6. Pierre le Verdier, ed., *Le Mystère de l'incarnation et la nativité de Notre Sauveur et
Rédempteur Jésus-Christ* (Rouen: Imprimerie de Espérance Cagniard, 1884–86).

7. Baron James de Rothschild, ed., *Le Mistére du Viel Testament* in 6 vols. (Paris: Librairie
de Firmin Didot, 1878–91), introduction, vol. 1, p. xviii.

centuries, the work of scholarship is not complete, for several immense mysteries have not yet been transferred from parchment to print.[8]

Arnoul Greban

Arnoul Greban, a contemporary of François Villon, was born in Le Mans in 1420 during the Hundred Years War, eleven years before Joan of Arc was burned. Greban moved to Paris during his youth to study at the university. Paris was a city in turmoil:

> Not until 1436 was Paris freed from English rule. This event brought some joy: there were magnificent processions through the streets, and in the next year, when the King made his entry into the city, there were great celebrations with mystery plays, and bonfires lit in the squares. But the country was in terrible shape. It was being ravaged by bands of un-paid men-at-arms, who ransacked anybody or anything they could lay their hands on.
>
> Then too there was a series of calamities: in the year before the En-glish left there occurred one of the coldest winters the city had ever known (it snowed steadily for forty days); two years later there was a famine in which many died; then there was a windstorm which knocked down houses, chimneys and trees; then came a smallpox epidemic which was said to have killed some fifty thousand people, mostly children; then there were several years when wolves, goaded by hunger, entered Paris and killed children and even women.[9]

Destined for a theological career, Greban found shelter in the cloisters of the Cathedral of Notre Dame during these difficult years and received his master of arts before 1444. He was then appointed to the post of organist of Notre Dame and master of the boys' choir. Greban saw productions by the

---

8. Major unpublished works include *The Acts of the Apostles* by Arnoul and Simon Greban: sixty-two thousand lines for five hundred characters. See Petit de Julleville, *Les Mystères*, vol. 2, pp. 461–65. *The Resurrection of Our Lord* by Jehan Michel: twenty thousand lines for one hundred fifty characters. See Petit de Julleville, *Les Mystères*, vol. 2, pp. 446–51. *The Passion of Jesus Christ* performed for twenty-five days in 1547 in Valenciennes: forty-five thousand lines. See Petit de Julleville, *Les Mystères*, vol. 2, pp. 422–24. *The Mystery of the Passion* was performed for eight days in 1501 in Mons. This production is not mentioned in Petit de Julleville, and the text is lost; most of the text could be recovered by collating the Greban and Michel *Passions* and the Mons *Promptbook*. See Gustave Cohen, ed., *Le Livre de conduite du régis-seur et le compte des dépenses pour le Mystère de la Passion joué è Mons en 1501* (Strasbourg: Im-primerie Alsacienne, 1924), introduction, p. xxxi.

9. Anthony Bonner, trans., *The Complete Works of François Villon* (New York: Bantam Books, 1960), pp. xvii–xviii.

Confrérie de la Passion of the Saint Genevieve dramas and possibly of *The Mystery of the Passion* by Mercadé. He himself was approached by Parisians, probably members of the Confrérie de la Passion, and was requested to write a new version of *The Mystery of the Passion*:

> Greban's play grew in the shadows and petty irritations of a cloistered existence, but it also took shape in an institution devoted to the worship of the Mother of God. It benefited from an excellent library and from the musical training of its author; it likewise shows signs, despite his competence, of considerable indebtedness to its predecessors; above all it reflects an overwhelming sympathy for the Virgin Mary.[10]

Greban's cyclic drama of thirty-five thousand lines of verse for four hundred characters must have been completed in time for one or more productions in Paris around 1450, for his reputation soon reached the provinces. Competition was intense among officials of the various provincial cities to produce the longest and most lavish production of a mystery:

> Another very curious story about a stroke of luck in the life of the ancient dramatists is the tale of the bourgeois from Abbeville going to find Arnoul Greban at his lodgings in Paris in 1452, and paying him the sum of ten gold crowns for a copy of the famous play of the Passion which he had already composed at the "request" of several Parisians. As this precious manuscript had been locked and sealed with the seals of the magistrate of Abbeville, "and placed in a chest in the sheriff's office of the said city, until we see these plays," other provincial cities must have imitated their sister from Picardy and thereby furnished the happy doctor with abundant resources.[11]

The Hundred Years War ended in 1453. Greban became bachelor in theology and worked on *The Acts of the Apostles* until his death in 1471. His younger brother, Simon Greban, Canon of the Cathedral of Saint-Julien in Le Mans, completed *The Acts of the Apostles*; it was the longest of the mysteries, containing sixty-two thousand lines for five hundred characters.

The Mystery of the Passion

Greban's original manuscript is entitled "The beginning and the Creation of the world in brief, by characters, the Nativity, the Passion and the

---

10. Frank, *Medieval French Drama*, p. 183. See her biographical material on Greban on pp. 182–83.

11. Gustave Cohen, *Histoire de la mise en scène dans le théâtre religieux français du moyen âge* (Paris: Librairie Honoré Champion, 1951), p. 190.

Resurrection of Our Savior Jesus Christ."[12] The authors of the three cyclic dramas that are each known simply as *The Mystery of the Passion*—Mercadé, Greban, and Michel—did not divide their texts by story titles. They divided their dramas into four days of performances of similar length. The three authors made divisions labeled "The First Day," and so on, for their respective texts of twenty-five thousand, thirty-five thousand, and thirty thousand lines. This division may have proved too ambitious for production purposes; directors had to take into consideration amateur actors, scenery changes, complex stage machinery, and restless audiences. The Mons directors divided the Mons *Passion* of 1501, based on the Greban text with portions by Michel and anonymous authors, into an eight-day production. The Valenciennes *Passion*, which was performed for twenty-five days in 1547, based on Greban and Michel with some new material, was a text of forty thousand verses, so that less than two thousand lines were performed each day.[13]

Greban's version of *The Mystery of the Passion* has a prologue containing the Creation. The First Day begins with the traditional Procession of Prophets, who lament in Limbo and await the Coming of Christ, followed by the Trial in Paradise, in which God agrees to send his Son to earth. Then the traditional Nativity story follows, including the Annunciation, the Journey to Bethlehem, the Nativity of Jesus, and the Adoration of the Shepherds. There are neither subtitles nor scenic divisions, but this part of *The Mystery of the Passion* corresponds to the parent text, the Saint Genevieve *The Nativity of Our Lord*. Greban's version continues with the Journey of the Three Kings, the Audience with King Herod, the Adoration of the Three Kings, and the Massacre of the Innocents. This portion corresponds to the Saint Genevieve *The Play of the Three Kings*.

Greban's cyclic drama is composed mostly in traditional octosyllabic couplets, although his versification shows an astonishing technical dexterity:

> Throughout, *rondeaux*, *ballades*, and other lyrical forms embellish the dialogue and, instead of being separated from it, as in the *Miracles of Notre Dame*, they are woven tightly into the texture of the drama. The delightful scene among the shepherds with its gay, complicated rhythms and harmoniously spaced refrains sounds as if it might have been danced as well as sung, and some of the *diableries*, with their refrains broken in midline and assigned to two different speakers, suggest similar eurhythmic gambollings and cavortings. In fact throughout the play Greban shows

12. Petit de Julleville, *Les Mystères*, vol. 2, p. 394.
13. Ibid., p. 418.

complete mastery of the divided line as well as of an endlessly varied vocabulary and strophic structure.[14]

Greban employs mnemonic lines: the last line of one speech rhymes with the first line of the next. This helps performers to remember their lines and to pick up their cues. Although the music for *The Mystery of the Passion* has been lost, it is very likely that the musically gifted Greban composed it: hymns in Latin and in French, motets, pastoral ditties, folk songs, drinking songs, diabolic rounds, or whatever else his characters require.

Greban's cyclic drama is cosmic and orthodox, attracting the faithful, offending no one. His soaring lyricism was enjoyed in numerous productions in French communities from the midfifteenth to the midsixteenth century. Although his drama has been called interminable, and lacking in dramatic conflict because the protagonist is a Man-God predestined to a sacrificial death, such comments must fairly pertain to the sacred mystery as a genre, not to Greban's mystery alone.[15] Civilizations have often found ways to celebrate the natural life cycle of death and rebirth in sacred drama, song, and dance; the Passion is incomplete without the Resurrection. Greban wrote a very compassionate mystery because he was devoted to Our Lady and because he lived through an era of war, disease, and famine. The Pietà, the scene in which the sorrowing Mother of God holds her dead Son on her lap after the Descent from the Cross, and wherein she delivers a long and exquisite lament, symbolizes *The Mystery of the Passion:*

> Much of the charm of Greban's work resides in its tenderness and the delicacy of its feeling. The author also combines a sense of the dramatic with a unique poetic lyricism, and technically his accomplishment far surpasses that of any of his predecessors. The role of Notre Dame in this play is exceptionally beautiful. . . . Greban's sense of the tragic conflict between the Virgin Mary's humanity and divinity, between her passionate maternity and her humility before God's will, is obvious everywhere.[16]

Mary seems to be as important a protagonist as Jesus in Greban's version of *The Mystery of the Passion.* Because she does not share her divine Son's perfect comprehension of God's will, she is more vulnerable, more capable of feeling interior conflict. *The Nativity* is certainly Our Lady's drama.

14. Frank, *Medieval French Drama*, pp. 186–87.
15. Paris and Raynaud, *Le Mystère de la Passion*, pp. xvi–xvii.
16. Frank, *Medieval French Drama*, p. 185.

The Nativity

Greban's *Nativity* is the traditional Christmas story based on the Books of Matthew and Luke; it recounts the sacred mysteries of the Incarnation and the Nativity. The protagonist is Mary, to whom Greban refers as Our Lady; she and her elderly husband, Joseph, struggle against poverty, political turmoil, and the dangers of the open road to protect the Babe entrusted by God the Father to their care. The spiritual and physical journeys of the Holy Family are watched with loving care by God the Father and his Heavenly Host, so that the Holy Family may be preserved from all harm by the Infernal Company, ruled by Lucifer. *The Nativity* was written for the French medieval polyscenic stage with juxtaposed mansions, as pictured in the Valenciennes miniatures: a wide rectangular stage with Heaven at stage right, Hell at stage left, and earthly locations in the middle.[17] The drama's cosmic religious significance is enhanced by the use of a stage plan that shows the intervention of the forces of Good and Evil in the lives of human beings:

> Concepts of spatial distance, therefore, and of the relative placement and proximity of the spiritual worlds of heaven and hell were savagely foreshortened and depicted emblematically, every concrete image having its universal analogue. For the playmaker this had been made easy by the readiness of theologians from St. Augustine onwards to compare God's creation with a theatre, and by the familiarity with which the audiences could be reckoned to approach allegorical representation of the invisible worlds of heaven, limbo and hell in sermons, art and literature. God and Lucifer viewed mankind's brief struggle in the theatre of mortal existence as audiences watched the actors strut and gesticulate upon the stage. It was thus as natural (and as easy) for an angel to descend to earth or for a devil to materialize from hell as it was for an actor to pass from Jerusalem to Damascus, from Israel to Italy or from Africa to Europe.[18]

The Holy Family's efforts to protect the Babe in his fragility are highlighted each time that God the Father must intervene with angelic messages to preserve his Son.

17. The Valenciennes miniatures by Hubert Cailleau depict the stage with its alignment of mansions in the Valenciennes *Passion* of 1547. See Élie Konigson, *La Représentation d'un Mystère de la Passion à Valenciennes en 1547* (Paris: Éditions du Centre National de la Recherche Scientifique, 1969), for comprehensive pictorial and diagrammatic documentation of this *Passion*.

18. Glynne Wickham, *The Medieval Theatre* (New York: St. Martin's Press, 1974), pp. 63–64.

God the Father introduces Mary: "Never did a more modest person live, more venerable or more sacred." Mercy, a Daughter of God, praises the Virgin in whose womb the Son of God will reside. Gabriel, an archangel who serves as messenger, greets Mary at the Annunciation in Nazareth with "sweet language." Mary's modest response to the Incarnation shows that her heart belongs entirely to God.

She treats her husband with respect and affection, and her pregnant cousin, Elisabeth, with consideration. However, there is an awkward moment when Mary returns from Elisabeth's house in a state of pregnancy. Joseph is shocked and angered because he and Mary have jointly vowed celibacy. Mary retreats to her room to pray: "Give me the virtue and the power to guard such a noble being well. A mystery takes place within me; I firmly believe it." God sends Gabriel to direct Joseph to remain with his wife, who bears the Messiah according to ancient prophecy. Joseph accepts his role as earthly protector of the Virgin and the Babe.

Mary does not complain during the Journey to Bethlehem, despite her advanced pregnancy and the worry that no shelter will be found in time. She patiently accepts God's will. The Holy Family settles, shortly before the Nativity, into a dilapidated shed, where she works and prays until Joseph asks her to rest. She replies, "Dear sire, do not pity me or allow any sadness into your heart, for joy and perfect gladness are in me very abundantly." She is alone during the Nativity, trusting in God the Father, who sends her a host of angels to sanctify the humble shed with light, music, and joy. She expresses gratitude: "Well must I in exultation, in devotion, admire this mystery when without any vexation, without my body having been damaged or soiled, I receive the fruit of my womb." Then she kneels to worship the Babe: "In this pitiful place thou hast a spotless birth, Son of high degree born of a humble mother. What more can I do? I announce thee in a clear voice, my gentle Babe, my true God and my Father."

When the shepherds arrive, they do not see the one angel who always remains with Mary, but they thank Mary for her "sweetness and mercy." She also receives the Three Kings with quiet dignity and thanks them for their gifts to her Son. She takes the Babe to be presented at the Temple in Jerusalem and shares the joy of his Nativity with the prophets there. She instantly obeys God's command to flee by night into Egypt to avoid Herod's wrath. Satan enrages Lucifer because he cannot corrupt Mary: "She is a rather young Virgin, the most courteous, the most beautiful, the sweetest, the kindliest, the most virtuous and the worthiest person who lives among the pure in heart today."

Greban must have felt great sympathy for Joseph, as both men, one a cleric and the other an elderly saint, dedicated their lives to the service of the Virgin and her Son. Joseph is presented as having the priestly virtues of poverty, celibacy, and obedience, but he has very human reactions to human dilemmas. Joseph has obeyed divine instructions to marry the young Virgin. When he takes his bride home and learns that she wishes to remain celibate, he graciously vows celibacy also, agreeing with her that their marriage will "arrive at a higher state." Joseph is patient when Mary leaves home for an extended visit to her cousin, Elisabeth. He is alarmed when she returns pregnant, because he fears that she has offended God by breaking her vow and sinned by committing adultery. This is not the reaction of a jealous husband. Joseph has accepted total responsibility for his young bride, and he is being protective of her virtue and her person. When Mary will not protect her honor by stating that she was molested, he decides to leave her secretly so that he will not be obliged to denounce her publicly as an adulteress. Yet he is disgusted with himself for doubting the virtue of the wife whom he dearly loves: "Oh mouth, guard what thou dost say! Shalt thou touch the honor of the sweetest maiden who reigns beneath Heaven, the sagest and most becoming, and in whose gracious mouth I have never heard an idle word?" After Gabriel explains the Incarnation to Joseph, he rushes to his wife to beg for forgiveness.

Circumstances compel Joseph to lead Mary on several arduous and dangerous journeys: from their home in Nazareth to Bethlehem, then to the Temple in Jerusalem, then home to Nazareth, then in flight to Egypt, and finally back to Nazareth. The polyscenic stage is ideally suited to simulated journeys; at several points during the drama, Joseph leads Mary on a donkey from one earthly location to another.

When Joseph and Mary settle into the uncomfortable Nativity shed, he sets up a manger and feeds the ox and donkey, makes a fire, and prepares for Mary a supper that she does not eat; then he goes to find swaddling clothes and milk. When Mary is alone, the Nativity is accomplished without being seen.[19] When Joseph returns, he finds the Mother of God worshipping a naked Babe. His astonished reaction is, "And I, poor unworthy sinner, seeing such a lofty mystery, and my sovereign Creator covered with our humanity, what can I best do but throw myself on the ground and adore the Babe?"

The Holy Family takes flight into Egypt to avoid the Massacre of the

---

19. Konigson, *La Représentation*, p. 79.

Innocents. The Apocryphal scene of the Fall of the Idols is based on the Gospel of Pseudo-Matthew:

> And happy and rejoicing they came to the region of Hermopolis, and entered an Egyptian city called Sotinen. And since there was in it no one they knew whom they could have asked for hospitality, they entered a temple which was called the "Capitol of Egypt." In this temple stood 365 idols, to which on appointed days divine honour was paid in idolatrous rites. The Egyptians of this city entered the Capitol, in which the priests admonished them, to offer sacrifices on so many appointed days according to the honour of their deity.
>
> But it came to pass that, when blessed Mary entered the temple with the Child, all the idols fell to the ground, so that they all lay on their faces completely overturned and shattered. Thus they openly showed that they were nothing. Then was fulfilled what was said through the prophet Isaiah: "Behold, the Lord rideth upon a swift cloud, and shall come into Egypt: and the idols of Egypt shall be moved at his presence, and the heart of Egypt shall melt in the midst of it."[20]

The antagonist to the Holy Family is fearsome King Herod, usurper of the throne of Judaea. As his only concern is for his sovereignty, he rages when the Three Kings ask him where the new King of the Jews has been born. The Three Kings, who are pious and discreet, listen with dismay to the rantings of the local tyrant. Then Herod pretends that he wishes to worship the Babe; he hopes that after the departure of the Three Kings either the incident will be forgotten or they will return to inform him where his enemy resides. When the Jews at his court warn him that the new King of the Jews has appeared in public and has been presented to reputable prophets at the Temple in Jerusalem, Herod orders the Massacre of the Innocents. God the Father punishes him severely: his own son is slaughtered by his soldiers, and Herod suffers a lingering and foul disease, eaten alive by worms, until he stabs himself.

God the Father, seated on an elevated throne, is surrounded by archangels, the Daughters of God, and choirs of angels composed of men and boys.[21] Although God the Father never descends to walk on earth, he keeps constant watch over all human activities. King Lucifer and the Infernal Company represent a gross parody of God the Father and the Heavenly

---

20. Edgar Hennecke, *New Testament Apocrypha: Gospels and Related Writings*, trans. R. McL. Wilson (Philadelphia: Westminster Press, 1963), vol. 1, pp. 412–13. The prophecy is in Isaiah 19:1.

21. Cohen, *Le Livre de conduite*, pp. xcvi–xcvii.

Host. Lucifer never leaves Hell, where he presides over a noisy throng of devils. Lucifer, known as the great devil or great dragon, may have been represented by a voice booming out of Hellmouth, a gigantic dragon's head. Messages from God the Father to the Holy Family and to the Three Kings are carried by archangels who walk or fly, according to the technical apparatus of each production.[22] Satan is both the messenger devil, warning Lucifer about the Nativity, and the Tempter, looking for souls to corrupt.

Balance and contrast are evident throughout the text. The shepherds are young and refreshingly innocent, whereas the Three Kings are mature and wise. The pompous decree of the Emperor is proclaimed by a drunken messenger. Doddering old Eliachin contrasts with the competent patriarch, Joseph. The innkeepers have no room for a poor family but find room for the Three Kings. The Nativity, a lofty mystery, takes place in a humble shed among animals. The mothers at the Massacre of the Innocents courageously try to defend their babes against arrogant, cowardly soldiers. Mercy, a Daughter of God who rejoices in the Redemption of humanity, contrasts with Salome, who promises Herod that she will slaughter many people. Idols fall before the true God.

The most sacred scene, the Nativity, is carefully constructed and staged. Eliachin, lost in the crowds in Bethlehem, is still searching for an inn. Joseph has helped with preparations in the shed and has gone out for needed supplies. Mary is alone during the darkest hour of the night, lying quietly on her couch of straw. The angels are trouping silently from Heaven to Bethlehem, their great wings and burning torches and candles making a beautiful procession. The shepherds call to each other in the dark from their various hilltops, keeping each other awake and alert against the wolves. Mary says, "Oh gracious God, remember me, as I have perfect belief in thee!" Then she places the Babe, represented by a doll, on the straw bed. The angelic host encircles the shed, filling it with light and joy. As Mary worships her Son, the angelic choir bursts into song; Joseph arrives to complete the tableau.

Suggestions for a Modern Production

The polyscenic stage with mansions juxtaposed requires that a series of short scenes be played in rapid succession. Stage directions in *The Nativity*

---

22. Angels flew at Valenciennes in 1547. See Konigson, *La Représentation*, pp. 77, 85.

from the Greban text are designated as (G), relevant stage directions from the Mons *Promptbook* of 1501 as (M). The following suggestions are based on my observations of blocking as implied by Greban's text. Since there are no wings, all performers may remain in view of the audience. Performers whose scene is not being played should be trained to sit still, freeze in a tableau, or travel very slowly without distracting attention from the action elsewhere. During turbulent crowd scenes, supernumeraries should fill the stage: the Daughters of God in Heaven (Peace, Justice, Truth, and Wisdom); townspeople in the streets of Bethlehem during the census taking; additional courtiers, priests, soldiers, and mothers with babes on earth; angels and devils; and patriarchs in Limbo. Performers should seem to be drawn from all medieval social classes; for example, angels are played by priests and devils are played by town ruffians. Massive participation creates a religious drama of cosmic proportions.

Since *The Nativity* was performed in a wide variety of indoor and outdoor locations in different cities and towns from the midfifteenth to the midsixteenth century, the stage plan must have varied. Because *The Nativity* was normally produced as part of the entire cycle of *The Mystery of the Passion* by Greban, the stage plan required some permanent structures and some mansions that could be changed between days of performance. My suggested stage plan for a modern production solves most of the blocking problems in the text, including frequent journeys. This stage plan, assuming a traditional rectangular stage dominated by Heaven at stage right and Hell at stage left, is a simplified version of the Valenciennes stage plans for the third through sixth days of that production:[23]

1. *Heaven* is a permanent two-story mansion with a neutral lower Hall of Heaven and an upper throne room where God the Father sits. The Three Kings may use the Hall of Heaven to represent their palaces, from which they depart on their journeys.

2. *Joseph's House in Nazareth* has two rooms. Mary's room, nearer to stage right, is equipped with a lectern facing Heaven; Joseph's room has a bed.

3. *The Mountain*, a temporary structure, is where Elisabeth lives because Luke 1:39–40 specifies that she lives in the hill country. The Annunciation to the Shepherds also takes place there.

23. Konigson, *La Représentation*, pp. 73–88.

4. *The Inn in Bethlehem* is used first for Sadoc's Inn, then for Eleazar's Inn. A room with three beds and a prie-dieu must be visible when the Three Kings take lodgings.

5. *The Nativity Shed in Bethlehem*, partially open, has a door.

6. *The Streets of Bethlehem*, used for the Massacre of the Innocents, are behind the Inn and the Nativity Shed.

7. *The Temple in Jerusalem*, a permanent structure, has an altar.

8. *Herod's Palace in Jerusalem*, a permanent structure with a throne, is also used by the Provost of Judaea.

9. *The Idols of Egypt*, an altar with idols, is behind the Sea.

10. *The Sea*, a temporary structure, is a shallow basin filled with water; it contains a sailboat.

11. *The Limbo/Hell/Hellmouth* complex is a permanent structure.

Live and prop animals were used. The text requires a donkey and an ox for the Holy Family, sheep and a dog for the shepherds, and caged turtledoves and pigeons for the Presentation at the Temple. Prop animals were less trouble whenever their use was possible; a real donkey was used at Mons, but the donkey at Valenciennes may have been a wooden one mounted on wheels. The Holy Ghost at the Annunciation was a carved dove, which descended in a sphere at Valenciennes. The Infant Jesus was represented by a doll; it is unknown how this doll suddenly made its appearance at the Nativity. Papier-mâché dolls filled with the blood of farm animals represented the babes at the Massacre of the Innocents. The evil soul of Herod may have been a black papier-mâché doll at Mons, which the devils appeared to cut out of Herod's bowels, although the doll was hidden under Herod's clothing. Angels did not fly at Mons in 1501, but they flew at Valenciennes in 1547. The star of Bethlehem, consisting of candles or fireworks, probably moved along a horizontal wire. The idols of Egypt may have fallen when the columns supporting their altar were pulled down. Costumes were a combination of Hebrew, Roman, Oriental, medieval, and liturgical garments. A close study of the scenery and costumes in the Cailleau miniatures of the twenty-five days of the Valenciennes production is invaluable in preparing a modern reconstruction of *The Nativity*.[24]

24. This paragraph is a summary of information from Cohen's introduction to the Mons *Promptbook* and from Konigson's commentary on the Valenciennes *Passion*. The twenty-five valuable miniatures and stage plan are in Konigson's book.

NOTES ON THE TRANSLATION

In preparing this translation, I used reference works, critical works, and primary sources. Besides French, English, French/English, and Latin/English dictionaries, I relied on the Larousse *Dictionnaire de l'ancien français* (Paris, 1968). I kept the King James Version of the Bible and the New Testament Apocrypha within reach, as well as the Gospels in Latin. The best general reference work on the French mysteries is Petit de Julleville, *Les Mystères* (Paris: Librairie Hachette, 1880). Twentieth-century critical works that illuminated the texts are Grace Frank, *The Medieval French Drama* (Oxford: Clarendon Press, 1954); D. D. R. Owen, *The Vision of Hell* (Edinburgh: Scottish Academic Press, 1970); and Ronald Vince, *Ancient and Medieval Theatre: A Historiographical Handbook* (Westport, Conn.: Greenwood Press, 1984).

Excellent material on the staging of the Mons and Valenciennes *Passions*, both of which were partly based on Greban's *Passion*, appears in Gustave Cohen, *Le Livre de conduite du régisseur et le compte des dépenses pour le Mystère de la Passion joué à Mons en 1501* (Strasbourg: Imprimerie Alsacienne, 1924), and in Élie Konigson, *La Représentation d'un Mystère de la Passion à Valenciennes en 1547* (Paris: Éditions du Centre National de la Recherche Scientifique, 1969). Staging is also discussed in A. M. Nagler, *The Medieval Religious Stage* (New Haven, Conn.: Yale University Press, 1976), and Gustave Cohen, *Histoire de la mise en scène dans le théâtre religieux français du moyen âge* (Paris: Librairie Honoré Champion, 1951). Iconographic evidence is in Gertrud Schiller, *Ikonographie der christlichen Kunst* (Gütersloh: Gütersloher Verlagshaus Gerd Mohn, 1968–1980).

Texts of French mysteries that I studied in detail before beginning this translation include the Chantilly mysteries edited by Gustave Cohen, *Mystères et moralités du manuscrit 617 de Chantilly* (Geneva: Slatkine Reprints, 1975); the Saint Genevieve collection edited by Achille Jubinal, *Mystères inédits du quinzième siècle* (Paris: Téchener, 1837); the Burgundian *Passion de Semur* edited by Émile Roy, *Le Mystère de la Passion en France du XIVe au XVIe siècle* (Dijon: Université de Dijon, 1903), *Revue Bourguignonne*, vol. 13; Mercadé's *Passion* edited by Jules-Marie Richard, *Le Mystère de la Passion* (Arras: Imprimerie de la Société du Pas-de-Calais, 1891); Michel's *Passion* edited by Omer Jodogne, *Le Mystère de la Passion* (Gembloux: Éditions J. Duculot, 1959); and the Rouen *Nativity* edited by Pierre le Verdier, *Le Mystère de l'incarnation et la nativité de Notre Sauveur et Rédempteur Jésus-Christ* (Rouen: Imprimerie de Espérance Cagniard, 1884–86). The text that I translated is taken from Gaston Paris and Gaston Raynaud's edition of *Le Mystère de la Passion d'Arnoul Greban* (Paris: F. Vieweg, Libraire-Éditeur, 1878). Omer Jodogne has edited a book by the same title (Brussels: Académie royale de Belgique, 1965–83).

An analysis of the origin of mysteries is in Glynne Wickham, *The Medieval Theatre* (New York: St. Martin's Press, 1974). Vast sources of information are Glynne Wickham, *Early English Stages: 1300–1660* (New York: Columbia University Press, 1959–81), and E. K. Chambers, *The Mediaeval Stage* (London: Oxford University Press, 1903). A translation of the Crucifixion portion of Greban's *Passion* appears in James Kirkup, *The True Mistery of the Passion* (London: Oxford University Press, 1962).

THE NATIVITY
by Arnoul Greban

Dramatis Personae

The Heavenly Host:
    God the Father
    Mercy, a Daughter of God
    Gabriel, Archangel
    Michael, Archangel
    Raphael, Archangel
    Uriel, Archangel
    Seraphim, men's choir
    Cherubim, boys' choir
The Infernal Company:
    Lucifer, ruler of Hell
    Satan, tempter on earth
    Astaroth, Devil
    Beelzebub, Devil
    Berich, Devil
    Cerberus, Devil
The Holy Family:
    Joseph
    Our Lady
    Elisabeth, cousin to Mary
    Eliachin, cousin to Joseph
The Shepherds:
    Aloris, first Shepherd
    Ysambert, second Shepherd
    Pellion, third Shepherd
    Rifflart, fourth Shepherd
    Garnier, fifth Shepherd
    Gombault, sixth Shepherd
The Three Kings and Company:
    Jaspar, King of Araby
    Melchior, King of Sabba
    Balthazar, King of Tharse

Anthiocus, knight to Jaspar
Celsander, knight to Jaspar
Cadoras, knight to Melchior
Polidorus, knight to Melchior
Lucanus, knight to Balthazar
Pirodes, knight to Balthazar

The Court of Herod:
Herod, King of Judaea
Salome, Herod's sister
Zorobabel, Pharisee
Gamaliel, scribe
Roboan, scribe
Adracus, count
Arphazac, knight
Hermogenes, knight
Agripart, soldier

Women at the Massacre of the Innocents:
Rap
Rachel
Andrometa
Arbeline
Medusa, nurse to Herod's son
Sabine, chambermaid to Herod's son

Other Characters:
Cirinus, Roman Provost of Judaea
Ligeret, messenger to Cirinus
Sadoc, first innkeeper in Bethlehem
Eleazar, second innkeeper in Bethlehem
The Sailor
Saint Simeon, prophet in Jerusalem
Anna, prophetess in Jerusalem
Theodas, priest in Egypt
Torquatus, priest in Egypt
The Actor

THE NATIVITY OF OUR LORD

God the Father with Gabriel and Michael

Scene 1. The Annunciation in Heaven

God the Father: A noble Virgin have I chosen of the blood and lineage of
David. Never did a more modest person live, more venerable
or more sacred. I wish her to become pregnant divinely without knowing a man; she will give birth as a Virgin to my beloved Son. She will nourish my Son with milk from her gentle
breasts.

Mercy: Oh blessed Virgin in whom such a flower will be placed, very
holy and precious handmaiden, how worthy thou art to be
praised! Thou wast created at a good time; for such nobility to
be placed in thee, thy womb is well disposed, when such a
Prince wishes to repose there.

God the Father: Gabriel, go to earth and explain this divine mystery to the
Virgin who will be mother of my dear Son. You bear certain
news, the strongest and highest news that was ever heard on
earth. The Virgin whom I have chosen is named Mary and is a
native of Galilee; you will find her in Nazareth. You will greet
her from me as you enter with sweet language, and then you
will prudently declare the message to her.

Gabriel: Creator of high Heaven, I will carry this noble and divine
message with a sincere heart. I will announce to her the sweetest and the most novel news that could ever come to earth.

Gabriel descends.   (M)

Cherubim: Let us on the right and on the left sing, and let us lead the
exultation, for this Annunciation rejoices us.

In Heaven great jubilation is made and they must sing.   (M)

Seraphim: When humanity is elevated to sovereign virtue,
The holy celestial court will know perfect joy.

A vertical bar indicates that the verse must be sung.

The Valenciennes Heaven and Nazareth

Michael:	Paradise will resound with very serene gladness, When humanity is elevated to sovereign virtue.
Raphael:	Our King will perfect humanity! He will clothe himself in flesh Within the pure Virgin his Mother.
Uriel:	When humanity is elevated to sovereign virtue, The holy celestial court will know perfect joy.

Scene 2. The Holy Family

Joseph, Husband of Our Lady:

Mary, if it does not displease you, may I declare my wishes to you?

Our Lady: Joseph, my gracious husband, tell me your thoughts.

Joseph: Very dear lady, it is true—my soul does not debate it—that by divine will I have been chosen, unworthy that I am, to be your husband or at least your guardian. May God grant that I guard you so well that my concern will bring merit to my soul! Notable lady, the law specifies that when two people come together in matrimony, before they cohabit, they must separate and see to their prayers for a certain time. I would prefer that we obey this law.

Our Lady: My wish is to obey the law and your will, my dear husband.

Joseph: The law is appropriate, and since it is also your wish, we will obey it.

Our Lady: This pleases me very well.

Joseph: Well then, Mary, let us part and retreat separately, so that we will have served God, from whom all good comes, for a certain time, so that he will confirm us in love and true union.

Our Lady: I will follow your advice diligently.

Scene 3. The Annunciation to Mary

Mary must go to the place of the Annunciation and pray here, her face toward Paradise. (M)

Our Lady: Here is a beautiful little chamber for serving God, my Creator. I would like to read my psalter, entire psalms one after the other. Now I am alone. First I pray for thy grace, God of justice who commands all, and I beg thee to give me such joy in contemplation that this consoling joy assures my salvation.

Gabriel: Hail, thou that art highly favoured, the Lord is with thee: blessed art thou among women. *Ave* for salutation; I salute thee with affection. *Maria*, Mary of devotion, very benign Virgin. *Gratia* by infusion of acceptable and worthy grace. *Plena*, pregnant by divine Virtue, when within thee resides *Dominus* by heavenly decree. Our Lord gives thee a great sign of love when he decides to reside within thee: *Tecum.*

Our Lady: I marvel to be thus greeted and I am troubled, as by an unaccustomed thing.

Gabriel: Fear not, Mary: for thou has found favour with God. And, behold, thou shalt conceive in thy womb, and bring forth a Son, and shalt call his name Jesus. He shall be great, and shall be called the Son of the Highest: and the Lord God shall give unto him the throne of his father David: And he shall reign over the house of Jacob for ever; and of his kingdom there shall be no end.

Our Lady: Oh beneficent Angel of God, you have given me lofty and admirable news. How shall this be, seeing I know not a man?

Gabriel: The Holy Ghost shall come over thee, and the power of the Highest shall overshadow thee: therefore also that holy thing which shall be born of thee shall be called the Son of God. And, behold, thy cousin Elisabeth, she hath also conceived a son in her old age: and this is the sixth month with her, who was called barren. For with God nothing shall be impossible. He is sufficient to do everything; without him no good is perfected. God is omnipotent, omniscient and infinite in his virtues.

The Annunciation and Visitation

Our Lady: *Ecce ancilla Domini.* Behold the handmaid of the Lord; be it
              unto me according to thy word. [1]

Organ music while the Holy Ghost descends. And then Gabriel goes away into Heaven.   (M)

Joseph, on his knees:
              Oh all good and perfect God, more than heart may compre-
              hend, I give you thanks for my loyal companion, whom you
              have given to me as my helpmate in my old age. Preserve
              Mary from harm and sorrow; preserve my wife and me as
              truly as when we were betrothed.

Gabriel: I must tell thee something important about Mary, the noble
              maiden, Joseph, so that thou dost not touch her. She has dedi-
              cated her virginity to God the Father with a clear intention.
              Leave her thus to persevere, and God, who rewards every
              good heart, will reward thee.

Joseph: Then may my body never touch hers. Mary has made a vow
              on a point that concerns me, for which reason she and I will
              rejoice.

Our Lady: Oh perfection of science, oh truth of the righteous path, oh
              power of pure Deity, never have I heard news that has rejoiced
              me more sweetly than this divine mystery. It is a work beyond
              Nature that I, humble creature, must give birth to my Creator.
              It is my blessing and my nourishment, which is promised to
              me by the stature of the Highest. My God, my good, my sal-
              vation, my recourse, my sole felicity, I humbly thank thee for
              this very high union which has already been accomplished
              within me; I have no doubt of it. Oh my true God of whom I
              am in such awe, such perfect faith grows in me because of
              what the Angel told me that I firmly believe that in my womb
              lies the Son of high Deity. Thou hast chosen me for a mystery
              of such great value that I bear thy Son in my womb! In this

              1. Luke 1:28–38.

joyous mystery, help me remain humble without increasing pride. Help me abstain from vices, and augment all virtues within me, so that the hour may come when thy dear Son may be born, and the very sweet fruit be presented to thee, from whom this flower has come.

Scene 4. The Vows of Chastity

Joseph: Beloved wife, I have learned about your vow through the excellent power of God, who has advised me. You have chosen the role of conserving virginity.

Our Lady: My dear sire, it is all that my heart desires.

Joseph: Then I vow to our Lord God that I will equally conserve mine as long as I live. On this point we will be of one mind.

Our Lady: Our marriage will be worth more and will arrive at a higher state. Dear husband, I would gladly go, with your gracious permission, to visit my cousin, Elisabeth, who lives at the mountain.

Joseph: If you wish to go, dear companion, I will not forbid you.

Our Lady: I have heard that she is pregnant. If she asks for none other than me to attend her, it will be a great courtesy on her part.

Joseph: Depart whenever you please, Mary, and may you return in joy.

Music. (G)

Scene 5. The Visit to Elisabeth

Our Lady: Elisabeth, honored lady, may God grant you a good day.

Elisabeth: Blessed art thou among women, and blessed is the fruit of thy womb. And whence is this to me, that the mother of my Lord should come to me? For, lo, as soon as the voice of thy salutation sounded in mine ears, the babe leaped in my womb for joy. And blessed is she that believed: for there shall be a performance of those things which were told her from the Lord.

Our Lady:	My soul doth magnify the Lord, And my spirit hath rejoiced in God my Saviour. For he hath regarded the low estate of his handmaiden: for, behold, from henceforth all generations shall call me blessed. For he that is mighty hath done to me great things; and holy is his name. And his mercy is on them that fear him from generation to generation. He hath shewed strength with his arm; he hath scattered the proud in the imagination of their hearts. He hath put down the mighty from their seats, and exalted them of low degree. He hath filled the hungry with good things; and the rich he hath sent empty away. He hath holpen his servant Israel, in re- membrance of his mercy; As he spake to our fathers, to Abraham, and to his seed for ever.[2]
Elisabeth:	Mary, your arrival pleases me greatly. Remain here from this hour for a good while with me.
Our Lady:	My only wish is to do your bidding, gracious cousin, and if I may do you any service, I beg you not to spare me.
Elisabeth:	Mary, your grace extends even unto me.

Scene 6. The Heavenly Host

Gabriel:	May praises be rendered unto you, Father of Heaven, powerful and wise. I have delivered your message, profitable to man- kind, to the Virgin full of grace, who has most worthily received it.
God the Father:	Her faith has not deceived her, for in her womb the fruit that I have promised to her has already been placed, for which cause great nobility will be bestowed upon her. Now, my Angels, you must visit her often. First I wish you to sing poems of joyous composition about the amiable news that Gabriel has announced, for this news requires great jubilation.

2. Luke 1:42–55.

Cherubim: Let us give glory to God and
Let us celebrate in the highest.
God, we praise you for such a noble event!

Seraphim: This noble mystery, good God,
Shows that you are favorable toward human beings,
Wishing to redeem those who, contrarily,
Are falling from grace.

Michael: Now they are on the path toward the destiny
That they ought to have:
For the divine King is so kindly to them
As to elevate them.

Raphael: Precious gift, gracious to see, precious Babe!
May the Virgin perceive and understand
How to guard him well.

Uriel: Let us compose lovely stanzas
And sweet melodies,
When to restore and purify human nature,
Our King humbles himself.

Gabriel: Oh, dear mistress! Oh, high princess!
Sovereign lady, thy great humility
Rejoices and refreshes our high court.
We hope that thou wilt restore humanity
To full glory: humanity whose wicked guilt
Robbed him of his nobility.

Music. (G)

Scene 7. The First Diablerie

Lucifer: Leap out of the black abysses, out of the dark infernal mansions, all stinking with fire and sulfur, Devils! Come out of your pit and out of the horrible regions. By thousands and by legions come to hear my case. Leave behind the chains and hooks, the gibbets and hanging thieves, stoked furnaces, biting serpents, dragons more blazing than a tempest. No longer

Hellmouth

burn your snouts and heads in making those metals run. For my sake make the whole hideous, infernal herd of swine come bounding and tottering with haste to throng together and hear my news.

Satan: Who is making that dreadful noise? Lucifer, King of the enemies, you howl like a famished wolf, whether you are singing or laughing.

Lucifer: Ah, Satan! My nobility and my great beauty have been transformed into deformity, my songs into lamentations, my laughter into desolation, my light into dark shadows, my glory into sorrowful rage, and my joy into inconsolable mourning. Nothing remains except my pride, which has never changed since the day when I was created up there in the everlasting Empire. If I speak falsely, may God always reign!

Satan: On one point you speak truly: never can you hope to find rest. But this is not the topic at hand, so we need not dwell on it.

Lucifer: Astaroth, sound the trumpet so that all the Devils in Hell leap out quickly.

Astaroth: If there remains any foot or paw that does not leap swiftly into the melee, may I have my vile and stinking substance burned.

Satan: Now come forth!

Here the trumpet. (G)

Astaroth: Lucifer, monarch by your own declaration, here are all the damned Devils in rows to hear your voice.

Lucifer: I am joyous when I see them overflowing from Hell in such a beautiful brigade. Devils, arrange yourselves and sing me a song in your horrible diabolic voices.

Astaroth: You will hear a motet of honor. Satan, thou shalt sing tenor, and I will attempt to sing baritone. Beelzebub and Berith will sing in harmony, and Cerberus will maintain the basso continuo, God knows how.

Lucifer:	Begin, my little Diablos; croak your notes and squall like urchins or old famished crows.
Berich:	Thou shalt begin, Beelzebub!
Beelzebub:	Begin!
Cerberus:	Begin!
Song together:	Hard eternal death is the song of the damned: Well does it bind us with its chain! Hard eternal death! We have deserved it and we surrender to it: Hard eternal death is the song of the damned.
Lucifer:	Stop! Rascals, you astonish me with your frightening cries; your voices blend too badly. Stop, by the Devil! I want to tell you news about which I am very worried. My Devils, it is true that by means of tricks and subtlety we, the inhabitants and citizens of the desolated region, found a way to lead human nature into great contrariness, when by our counsel we moved mankind with desire to touch the fruit of life, for which reason the whole generation of mankind must descend into Hell. But I have great doubts about one point: that someone will deliver them, or that whoever it may be will clear their record in order to undo our power.
Astaroth:	Deliver them? That can never be done. Human souls have never departed from Hell, but every day fresh heaps of them arrive.
Lucifer:	Astaroth, be quiet; thou art still a novice. Satan, thou art a useful beggar. I want to hear thy terrible voice. Satan, does it seem to thee impossible to deliver our prisoners who are cloistered here in Limbo, deprived of glory?
Satan:	Master, my claws entrap some wicked and sad people of whom we are very assured, for they will never depart. But as for the other group of prophets and patriarchs, I fear that they will escape from our borderlands some day.
Berich:	Never will they get out of prison!

Lucifer:	Satan, when thou runnest and goest throughout the world, dost thou ever look at the Scriptures to know if the Scriptures ever make any mention of our adventures?
Satan:	The prophets have prophesied marvels: that a strong King will arise who will despoil our Hell. I do not know if it is true or not, who he will be, or what his name is, but the Scriptures certainly make fine speeches about him.
Lucifer:	Do you know why I ask this? Never do I hear those prophets and patriarchs cease their loud lamenting and calling for help. I do not know from whence help could reach them, nor who would be able to even remember them, considering their great offense, and that God has passed sentence on mankind that even God cannot and must not revoke. However, in order to better apply power and guard our rights, Satan will go strike a blow on earth. At least, if perchance there were born a man of virtue so perfect that by him the transgressions of humanity ought to be redeemed, Satan will tempt him to do evil. For if Satan can undermine him so much that he is corrupted by sin, that man's act of redemption will be destroyed; for no matter what ransom he pays for humanity, it will be worthless. He will be unworthy to make satisfaction.
Satan:	I will perform every task of visitation on earth, without long protests.
Astaroth:	Since thou art so devoted, no other courier is needed.
Satan:	But before I leave, I must have a blessing by your ugly paw, so that my efforts will be successful.
Lucifer:	Mayest thou lead the Devils in such a direction that, at thy return, great dragons may escort thee pleasantly back, burning like a furnace fire!

Music. (G)

Scene 8. The Pregnancy of Mary

Joseph, being in his house:

Oh Creator of high degree, who has formed me in thine image and has given me understanding, give me the will and the courage in this human pilgrimage to serve thee faithfully. If I have been lacking in anything, or if I have not served thee ardently as a wise man should, give me the heart to cleanse myself. I who have already come into old age, as much as any man of my lineage, rejoice that God has given me in my old age so holy and so good a wife. She is the kindliest person under Heaven. But I am concerned that she has not returned, for she has already remained away for a long time.

Here remind Mary to raise her belly to show that she is pregnant. (M)

Our Lady:	Elisabeth, dear cousin, since God has permitted you to come to delight and joy, it is time for me to set out on the road to return to my husband, lest he be upset at my long delay.
Elisabeth:	Mary, blessed Virgin, I thank you a hundred thousand times for the goodness and courtesy you have shown me.
Our Lady:	My dear cousin, my companion and my sweet friend, I have helped you with a sincere heart. My prayer is raised to God that he may give you such good health that what I have done for you is nothing. Farewell, cousin.
Elisabeth:	Farewell, my lady and my dear mistress. My heart weeps at our parting, since I shall be far away from your sweet self.
Our Lady:	Farewell, Elisabeth.
Elisabeth:	Farewell, my lady and my dear mistress. I pray God that you may soon see the precious fruit that reposes in your womb with delight and joy in your eyes.

Remind Mary to go toward Joseph having her belly large as has been said. (M)

Joseph: I think—I suppose—I see Mary returning. I am no longer in doubt—it is she. I know her well. My darling, my hope, my well-being, you are welcome home! Your presence is worth much to me.

Mary must approach Joseph, then she speaks. (M)

Our Lady: My amiable and gentle husband, may our Sovereign, true God, give you joy.

Joseph: My darling, my sweet wife, my tender companion, has it always been well with you since you left here?

Our Lady: Yes, sire, God be thanked, and it still is. And you?

Joseph: It has been so well that I could not hope for better. Even if evil were to befall me, your presence would greatly rejoice me; there is no more beautiful contentment in this world. How is our cousin Elisabeth?

Our Lady: She is now in the path of all beauty. She is increased by a handsome son named John, at whose birth all that noble country demonstrated great rejoicing.

Do not let Joseph forget to show his astonishment upon beholding that Mary is pregnant. (M)

Joseph: I had not noticed this marvel. How, Mary, dear wife? Your belly has greatly grown. How did this happen? Are you show-ing yourself thus as a pretense, or are you in reality pregnant? How, Mary? You know that since I have had you as my wife, I have never touched you. With a common will we have vowed virginity, to which I do not wish contradiction. Because of this, you cannot say that any fruit begotten in you comes from my loins, both because of our common vow and because of my age, which repudiates begetting of children. Oh lady of devotion, the sweetest and the wisest who lives in this world, you are pregnant for certain! It is clear. What sin took place? At least, if you met with mishap, excuse yourself for your honor's sake.

Our Lady: My husband and my dear lord, do not be enraged against me.
You and I have jointly vowed virginity, a praised virtue, which
vow I have not broken, but I have maintained it without con-
straint, of a free and open will.

Joseph: Alas! Your belly gives me matter to believe the contrary. It is
time for us to retreat to our chambers for the night. Go to
bed, if you do not mind, Mary, and tomorrow you will hear
what is weighing on my heart.

Our Lady: May God in Heaven, who created us, remain in your
company!

Joseph: And may he guard you, Mary, in very good prosperity. I will
go away on the other side to rest in my chamber.

Joseph turns away.   (M)

Scene 9. The Suspicions of Joseph

Our Lady: Oh good God, thou who does wish to compose this beautiful
world for thy pleasure, and then to place humanity in it so
that humanity may take sustenance there, thou dost know that
by high union thy dear Son reposes in my womb. Give me the
virtue and the power to guard such a noble being well. A mystery takes place within me; I firmly believe it. This Babe is the
precious Son of God, true heir of Deity who, in order to take
the form of humanity, wishes to imprint himself within me.
Oh very perfect humility, no mouth can express thee! Can
Nature express what surpasses all her laws? Can humanity
understand the high and divine deeds? But thou, good God,
who foresees and knows all deeds before they are done, think
of my case. As thou canst see, I am in need and I require thy
help.

Joseph: My worries about Mary, my holy spouse whom I have found
thus pregnant, cannot be laid aside. I do not know whether or
not she has been harmed. Oh lady of great renown, Virgin of
flowering virtue, very prudent wife Mary, the humblest and

wisest of all women, thou dost put strong doubts in my heart.
I do not know thy situation. Know? What am I saying? It is
necessary, since a Child has been conceived in her womb, that
she has committed adultery, for the Child has not come from
me. She has not kept her promise; she has broken her marriage
vows. Broken? What art thou saying, hard-hearted man? She
is too holy a person to be scandalized. Oh mouth, guard what
thou dost say! Shalt thou touch the honor of the sweetest
maiden who reigns beneath Heaven, the sagest and most becoming, and in whose gracious mouth I have never heard an
idle word? Hast thou said that one with so sweet a face and so
prudent a character can commit adultery? Thou liest; it is impossible for her. Lie? Yet I clearly see her condition. She is
pregnant, and from whom would that Child come? It is essen-
tial to attest that, under the law, she has committed the vice of
adultery, since I am surely not the father. God, what horror!
And shall I believe it? Nay, I lie. Yet I do not know. She has
been away from here for three entire months, and at the end of
the third month I have received her home, very pregnant. Did
some villain deceive her or force her? In brief, I do not know
what to think. But I have resolved that, because of the great
perfection that I have truly seen in her, as long as I live, I will
not believe that she is pregnant through her own negligence.
Here is what I resolve to do to remove myself from this dangerous situation: I will prepare my bags, and tomorrow at day-
break I will depart very suddenly. Yes, and I will leave her by
herself. Therefore, I pray the immortal Essence to watch over
her and guard her from evil.

Here Joseph goes to bed. (G)

Scene 10. The Annunciation to Joseph

God the Father: Gabriel.

Gabriel:	Powerful Father, whatever you wish will be accomplished.
God the Father:	I have given careful consideration to Joseph's predicament. He is a just man of integrity who has a number of doubts concerning the blessed Virgin. He is determined to secretly leave her. Explain to him the Virgin's sacred pregnancy and her great nobility, and tell him that he must not leave her for any reason, for I have placed her under his protection.
Gabriel:	This will be accomplished according to your will, divine Father.

Music. (G) Remember here that organ music must be played while Gabriel goes toward Joseph.   (M)

Gabriel:	Joseph, thou son of David, fear not to take unto thee Mary thy wife: for that which is conceived in her is of the Holy Ghost. And she shall bring forth a Son, and thou shalt call his name Jesus: for he shall save his people from their sins.[3] Now I depart, and do not forget.

He must return into Heaven.   (M)

Joseph:	Oh high noble Power, true adored Majesty, how shall I make amends for the offense of disbelief that I committed sinfully against my loyal wife? Oh holy royal maiden, most prudent of women, why didst thou not remove this doubt? Why didst thou not tell me? Alas! Why didst thou not announce this mystery to me, that thou hast been chosen to be mother of the sweet Christ promised by holy Scriptures? Oh Mary, thou hast a strong will and a constant heart; thou didst keep this secret enclosed with a fine clasp, firmly locked in thy heart. Thou hast prudently kept these divine secrets well hidden because they must be neither revealed nor declared by any human mouth, but left to highest Virtue to reveal. Yet I am not content with the laments that I know how to make until I have begged pardon for this, in seeing thy sweet face.

3. Matthew 1:20–21.

Music. **(G)** *Do not let Joseph forget to return to Mary at the end of his speech, at the moment when he knows that she is watching him.* **(M)**

Joseph:	Mary, to make amends, I greet you with a good and fine day.
Our Lady:	Dear husband, may God increase your fortunes in a saintly manner. You have risen early; tell me from what cause the occasion arises.
Joseph:	Ah, lady, there is good cause. I come to you, dear wife, humiliated in body and soul, to beg mercy for the offense that I did to your innocence, and to confess that I doubted your virginity when I found you pregnant. Thank you for your courtesy, Mary, my joy, my love. Never will I doubt another day. The Angel has made me certain, and has given me a revelation of the divine mystery that resides within you.
Our Lady:	I praise God for this, since it pleases him to make you certain. The mystery is noble and lofty; I pray God that he may perfect it according to his good will.
Joseph:	Amen, according to his grace, and may he give us great joy in this Child!

They must sit in their house in Nazareth. **(M)**

Scene 11. The Decree of the Emperor

Cirinus, Provost of Judaea:
I must accomplish my duty concerning the decree in my hands from my master, the Roman Emperor, Augustus.

Ligeret:
This is the real business of a messenger:
No decree matters to him as much
As eating well and drinking well.
This is the real business of a messenger!
Is there some new decree to proclaim? Show it to me, and I will proclaim it sooner than a magpie makes a somersault.

Cirinus:	Take this decree and go away throughout all the land of Judaea, traveling far and wide, to proclaim it to everyone.
Ligeret:	Let me study it first and I will do marvels.
Cirinus:	Always beware of the bottle; watch thy drinking and the dangers of the road.
Ligeret:	So that I may have a better memory and proclaim the decree more clearly, I want to take a little nip before I set forth.
Cirinus:	Be off with thee and proclaim thy decree. Thou dost dream too much of food and drink.
Ligeret:	This is the real business of a messenger: No decree matters to him as much As eating well and drinking well. This is the real business of a messenger!

Music.   (G)

Scene 12. The Proclamation

Ligeret:	Hear ye, hear ye! May all true subjects of the noble Roman Empire listen to my words. You must know that the Emperor, who is sovereign over all men, wishes to know the total number of all the people in the world. Men, women and children must obey him. All the tribes must be counted, to determine whether the Emperor should receive more or less taxes. Let each of you return to the city of your birth, where clerks await you to write down all your names for an accurate census. And the disobedient will arrive at an evil fate, doubt me not.
Joseph:	Mary, dear wife, you have heard what the Emperor commands.
Our Lady:	Since it is thus decreed, my dear lord, we will obey. We will go to present ourselves in Bethlehem, the great and beautiful city of David wherein we were born and raised.
Joseph:	Ah, lady, my heart is distraught to think that you must travel, for your season is near. I fear that the journey will be woeful for you.

Our Lady: My dear lord, have no doubts; God will aid us.

Joseph: My beloved wife, since it is thus, let our donkey carry you. We will travel carefully. Since we do not have as much money as we will need, we will take along this ox to sell to help pay for the journey.

Our Lady: Whatever pleases you must please me.

Joseph: Now I am going to obtain the necessities for our voyage.

Scene 13. The Journey to Bethlehem

Eliachin: Joseph, my dear relative, I fear going to Bethlehem on such short notice. The voyage is long and arduous; too much harm can come to us on the open road. I do not know what caused the Provost to burden us so, and to give us such a command that cannot bear any fruit.

Joseph: Eliachin, I am instructed that the great Provost of Judaea has not proclaimed this decree by his own authority, but it is the dreaded Emperor who has transmitted this decree to him. If you would like, Mary and I will travel with you.

Be sure that the donkey on which Mary goes to Bethlehem is ready, when the proper time comes, and also the ox. *(M)*

Joseph: Now please help me to lift my wife onto this donkey.

Eliachin: By your grace, may it please you to make such a request. Oh very noble and honest lady, you are greatly weakened by pregnancy and near your term. May you deliver your Babe with joy! It is a great sin to place the burden of this voyage on you, and truly, I am sorry for you.

Then they put Mary on the donkey and they depart from Nazareth and go away to Bethlehem. *(M)*

Joseph: Now let us be on our way over mountains and plains. May the majesty of dreaded God be pleased to provide for our safety!

Here they go away into Bethlehem. Music. (G) Then they go away and Joseph leads the donkey by the bridle and Eliachin leads the ox. Organ music. (M)

Scene 14. The Census Taking

Ligeret:	Sire Provost, may Mohammed protect you and maintain you in his friendship! I have proclaimed the decree loudly in every city.
Cirinus:	Thou art a clever messenger. It is time for us to make preparations for the census taking.
Ligeret:	Consider providing your clerks with much parchment. So many people are coming on the roads that I have never seen such a multitude! Everyone is making it his study to retreat into his natal city; there is no one so great that he dares to refuse.
Cirinus:	I am delighted because this is a sign that our Emperor rules powerfully and that he is very well obeyed.

Scene 15. The Search for Lodgings

Joseph:	Now let us praise the clemency of God, to whom we are beholden; we have come into Bethlehem at the peril of our lives.
Eliachin:	Joseph, we agree that it is essential to ask for lodgings first. People are accustomed to finding lodgings as soon as they arrive, and once their places are secured, those who come afterward are deprived.
Joseph:	We have arrived very late, for the city is already overflowing with people in such a great assembly that people do not know where to stretch out and sleep.
Our Lady:	God will held us; let us place our hope in him.
Eliachin:	Never have I seen such a crowd since I was born! One does not know where to find lodgings for his money.

Joseph:	Dear cousin, be diligent; go see if we may have lodgings. Mary and I will be nearby, searching for lodgings on the other side.

Then Eliachin must be warned to go from inn to inn, without speaking, to ask for some place for them to lodge; and he must hurry back in order to say his speech.   (M)

Eliachin:	I have been to several inns, but I will search in over a hundred inns until I find a decent place for this good young lady.
Joseph:	Eliachin, I feel profound pity for her, I promise you. It does not matter so much for me; one night passes quickly.
Eliachin:	The good lady is tired. This is very hard on her. But let me boldly handle this; I will find her a place somewhere.
Joseph:	I will also try to find a place. Mary, if it does not distress you too much, follow me at a leisurely pace.
Our Lady:	I pray to God that it may please him to rescue us from this danger!
Eliachin:	Dear sire, could we lodge here to pass the night? Could a place be made ready for us, for our money, I beg you?
Sadoc, Innkeeper:	
	You may not. The place is filled; that's too bad for you. You see here the mob inside, and yet you ask for a place! You must not loiter here so long.
Eliachin:	I start to understand the situation: poor people have no help today. Alas, sire, look everywhere to see if there is not some little retreat, some little chamber. It will not be too lowly and insufficient for us.
Sadoc:	Don't you believe me? Even if I had a place for you, you would still not lodge in it. This is not a hospital of charity; it is an inn for gentlemen on horseback, and not for such lowly people. Go sleep out in the fields, and clear out of my house immediately!

Eliachin:	Ah, sire! You have no reason to be wrathful. Who is bothering you? Pardon me; I take my leave.
Joseph:	For God's sake, may we be lodged here? May we have a place, brother?
Sadoc:	Nay, by my soul, worthy father, since I do not wish to evict others.
Joseph:	Alas, sire, if it is possible, show us a little friendship. Look for a moment in pity upon my wife, who is so very pregnant and pale with fatigue, and then see if there is anything you can do to help her.
Sadoc:	I do feel pity in looking at her, a lady of such prudent bearing. But, worthy father, you know very well that those who take rooms early have the right to them. If I tried to give you a place, I would have to evict someone else. The custom is very ancient.
Joseph:	My host, be assured that I do not wish to find my own comfort by putting other people out. Let the rights of each person be respected. Therefore, for God's sake, please look for some place, without distressing any soul, where this good lady and I may stay two or three nights.
Sadoc:	No matter how much I search, no matter how much I have the goodwill to offer you some kindness, I cannot find any chamber or room that is not completely full. I do not know what to do, unless you wish to make use of an old shed here.
Joseph:	May we please see it? Perhaps we will be comfortable there.
Sadoc:	Look at this shed, fine friends. Enter; the door is open. It is crumbling and uncovered. This is not a lodging at all, God knows.

Here he must indicate the shed.   (M)

Joseph:	That's true, but while awaiting something better, we must accept whatever we find.

Sadoc:	That's the point. Then will you stay here?
Joseph:	Yes.
Sadoc:	The place is not worth much.
Joseph:	Lady, our place has been found. Take courage and descend. One could find a better or a worse place than this.
Our Lady:	May our Lord be praised for all the bounties he sends us!
Sadoc:	This is not a place of honor.

Scene 16. The Nativity Shed

Joseph:	May our Lord God be praised! And even if the place were worth less, it would be better to find shelter than to remain out on the road at night, cold and in danger. At least this shed is peaceful enough.
Our Lady:	May our Lord God be praised for all the good things he sends to us. I hope to see better times when our Lord God pleases.
Joseph:	Dear lady, we will do without. For me, this is comfortable enough, but for you, it is insufficient. High Majesty knows this. Oh, loyal Virgin, treasured receptacle of Deity, sweet flower of virginity wherein the very gentle Messiah lies, I see that you must have a pitiful dinner here and lodging of poor value. I pray God to sanctify this place in highest Heaven for your sake.
Our Lady:	We will endure all patiently.
Joseph:	My very dear and benign wife, rest near this fire and make yourself comfortable. I will put our ox and donkey together in this corner, and I must feed them, for it seems to me that they are in danger of starvation. Then I will go look for something for us to eat.

They tether the donkey and the ox. (M)

Our Lady:	Attend to their provisions first.

Joseph: Both of them are well tethered. I will set up a manger for them over here on this side, as well as I can, to set their fodder apart. Now turn around, donkey; turn your muzzle toward the manger and eat with appetite. You have not had enough.

Then Joseph pretends to give them something to eat, and then he goes away behind Our Lady; and he does not return at all toward her until he is signaled, and he is not at the Nativity.   (M)

Scene 17. The Shepherds

Aloris, First Shepherd:
It is a rather mild season
For Shepherds, thanks be to God.

Ysambert, Second Shepherd:
If the Shepherds are right,
It is a rather mild season.

Pellion, Third Shepherd:
I could not remain indoors
And miss this beautiful weather!

Aloris:
It is a rather mild season
For Shepherds, thanks be to God.

Ysambert:
Fie on wealth and worry!
There is no life so well fed
That it is worth the Shepherd's life.

Pellion:
People like us who frolic say,
"Fie on wealth and worry!"

Rifflart, Fourth Shepherd:
I am one of your own kind
With my little flowery beard.
When I have my fill of bread, I cry,
"Fie on wealth and worry!"

Aloris:
There is no life so well fed
That it is worth the Shepherd's life.

Ysambert:	Is there any gaiety sweeter Than seeing these beautiful fields, And these gentle grazing lambs Leaping in the beautiful meadow?
Pellion:	People talk of great lordships With dungeons and powerful palaces. Is there any gaiety sweeter Than seeing these beautiful fields?
Rifflart:	When my bread safe is furnished With thick and nourishing loaves, With my flute I make you a song. There is no better symphony!
Aloris:	Is there any gaiety sweeter Than seeing these beautiful fields, And these gentle grazing lambs Leaping in the beautiful meadow?
Ysambert:	Shepherds have a good life while they guard their sheep; they play their bagpipes and sing merry songs. And the sweet Shepherdesses pluck sweet-smelling herbs and beautiful flowers. Whoever could, would live a hundred years as a Shepherd!
Pellion:	The Shepherd who has a locked bread box is a little king. What more does he need? He has his wicker hat, dagger, and dear Shepherd's crook. He wears a handsome apron and shoes of curried leather. May he make good cheer; he's a little king.
Rifflart:	The Shepherd has his scissors, knife, thick winter mittens, nut box, wooden calendar, lard and peas, heavy coat. Does he lack anything? Thick ankle boots, two or three flageolets, choice drums and flutes, and a leash for Briet, his great dog. If I listed all his gear, it would take me months.
Pellion:	Let us make camp here for a while where we can watch our sheep grazing. There is no milder place for us unless we climb higher.
Rifflart:	Eight days ago I overheard that—I do not know what great lord—what is his name?

Pellion:	The Emperor?
Ysambert:	In truth, it's the Emperor of Rome, who is making every man enroll on his lists.
Aloris:	Enroll? But for what purpose? Is it to fight a battle?
Rifflart:	Truly, or to pay a heavy tax, which will be hard for us.
Pellion:	Whatever chance may bring! If people are arriving from so many places, our sheep will be sold so much dearer in Bethlehem and elsewhere.
Ysambert:	It is time to put on warm clothes, for at night we must stay awake and watch over the flocks, each man by himself.
Aloris:	I am all ready.
Rifflart:	So am I, to keep guard until the morning bells.
Pellion:	When I have put on my ankle boots and my thick mittens, even if it were to freeze the toads, I would not fear whatever cold spell may come.
Ysambert:	We are ready; let each man take his place. Whoever sees the wolf will make noise.
Aloris:	If he comes, there will be entertainment! Let each man guard against making mistakes.

Music.   (G)

Scene 18. The Holy Family

Joseph:	Oh dear wife, would you please have a little dinner? And do not work so much. It is not good to be too burdened. You are alway at work or in prayer, but human nature is not powerful enough to do this. Also you, who are heavy with child, have no need to work.
Our Lady:	Joseph, I make preparations willingly, and I have an urgent reason, for the time is extremely near for my blessed delivery. I think that soon the hour will be consummated.
Joseph:	Oh lady of great renown, virtuous and good above all women, this place is not suitable, but vile and badly outfitted. But

since the incarnate Essence has thus ordained his time of birth, and selects this place for his birth, may God be praised a thousand times! And yet, when I see you in this state, I cannot cease lamenting.

Our Lady: Dear sire, do not pity me or allow any sadness into your heart, for joy and perfect gladness are in me very abundantly. Instead of fear, I have certain assurance of not being burdened, because of my conserved virginity, so that childbirth will be accomplished without causing me any distress. Instead of heaviness, I have lightness. Instead of weakness, I have sound health. For my body and soul are in accord, it seems to me, and I do not sense anything that grieves me.

Joseph: Now I pray to God that he may let you give birth quickly, so that we may humbly receive the precious fruit. Mary, I am going to go provide what will be needed to help you in this delivery. My power is very small, but nevertheless, I have a good appetite for showing you every diligent care.

Here Our Lady lies on her couch; Joseph goes to take care of little things for the Babe.   (G)

Scene 19. The Rejoicing in Heaven

God the Father: The time has come that my providence has determined and ordained for my dear Son Jesus to be born, mothered by the noble and sacred Virgin. And so that such a noble Nativity may be better consecrated, Angels, sing a beautiful song in voices sweet and melodious to lead the abundant rejoicing.

Then let great joy be shown in Paradise; and let them sing that which follows.   (M)   Song of the Angels all together: (G)

> The celebration begins, now that the Lord
> Of the World and Savior must be born.
> To his majesty be praises and honor!

> It is humility on the part of the Creator
> To take human form, and for Deity
> To join humanity as servant to humanity!

God the Father: To show our nobility and highness on this blessed night, I wish a great part of the angelic host to go to that place where the Virgin is lying. The place that is insufficient for such a great occasion will be furnished with noble light. Our treasured friend must be comforted and made perfect with true joy, and she must be nobly attended. You will all bear her company, so that the Nativity may be reverently accomplished, as is worthy of this mystery.

Michael: Sovereign divine Essence, we will accomplish your command, and we will console the Virgin by bringing reverent homage.

Gabriel: Sovereign King, all that you have spoken will be accomplished, with very great and perfect will. This is right, very wise Judge.

God the Father: Gabriel, our dear messenger, as soon as the Child is born, let the news be announced to the Shepherds of the country who are guarding their flocks. For it pleases me that they should be informed of this joyous birth.

Gabriel: Gracious God, we are filled with grace in obedience to you.

Here they descend with burning torches and candles and go to the place where Our Lady lies. (G) Then Gabriel descends with several other Angels and they go to the place of the Nativity, and meanwhile, the Shepherds speak. (M)

Scene 20. The Shepherds at Night

Aloris: Guard well against the wolves; guard, Shepherds, be on a good guard!

Ysambert: But you who command us, guard well against the wolves. Guard!

Pellion: Listen on your side. Here I am setting a good guard!

Rifflart: Guard well against the wolves, Shepherds; be on a good guard!

Aloris: Whoever has doubts, let him be on guard! And even if I shiver with cold, I do not think at all about sleeping until the morning comes.

Scene 21. The Nativity

Our Lady: Oh gracious God, remember me, as I have perfect belief in thee!

Here God is born. (G)   Here the little Jesus must appear, born; and Mary is before him, on her knees. (M)

Our Lady: Oh powerful magnificence, oh pity, oh compassion, oh rich treasure of clemency, oh divine Incarnation! Well must I in exultation, in devotion, admire this mystery when without any vexation, without my body having been damaged or soiled, I receive the fruit of my womb. My God, my gentle King, in whom alone I believe, my only recourse and refuge, all my heart praises thee and thanks thee for this great kindness, infinite Power, that I receive from thee.

Then a great melody must be made, at the place of the Nativity, and great light. (M)

Michael: Angels, let us arrange ourselves in order, and let us sing a pretty motet at the birth of the One who is Sovereign of thrones.

Song of the Angels together:

	Welcome to thee, highest King!
	At a good hour thou art made man:
	We venerate thee, we praise thee,
	We adore thee, Infant of great value!
Gabriel:	We hope that through thee, we will be understood by humanity.
Michael:	Thy holy Nativity has brought us glorious spirits.

Angels at the Nativity

Uriel:	The time has come to separate humanity from harsh fear, so that humanity may come to glory.
Raphael:	Blessed be the dear resting place, the holy chapel that contained thee.
Seraphim:	In thy coming, humanity will be whole and restored again.
Cherubim:	Adorned Virtue, adored Power, we proclaim thee true God.

Music.   (G)

Scene 22. The Adoration of Mary and Joseph

Joseph must approach on the third line of his speech and say, marveling: "Oh glorious Trinity! etc." And at the end of this speech, where he says: "My highest Creator, my only Judge," he must then be on his knees before the Babe.   (M)

Joseph:	I have found good provisions, so it is time for me to return. I hope that I have not been away too long, as Mary will be needing me. Oh glorious Trinity! What do I see at this hour? I perceive an Infant crying, lying all naked on the straw, and the mother is on her knees in front of the Babe, adoring him with great reverence, as the divine Presence before whom every knee bends. And I, poor unworthy sinner, seeing such a lofty mystery, and my sovereign Creator covered with our humanity, lying in such fragility, what can I best do but throw myself on the ground and adore the Babe? My highest Creator, my only Judge, Infant, so do I perceive thee.
Our Lady:	My beloved Infant, my very dear offspring, my wealth, my happiness, my only Child, my tender flower whom I carried for nine months and engendered with my own blood! I have given birth as a Virgin to thee. This has given me the certain hope that no soul can compare with thee in power. So I adore thee and proclaim thee in a clear voice, my gentle Babe, my true God and my Father.

Joseph:	Thou art the Saviour of the world, Infant in whom all good is abundant and pure by imperial power. In thee our wealth overflows; thou art the cornerstone and the foundation wherein our special hope is grounded. For from the virginal womb thou hast loyally taken the royal scepter, in order to judge this fine world round. As thou art our very just feudal Judge, I worship thee with deep fear.
Our Lady:	I was highly comforted in my heart to receive thy sweet Annunciation, and I was delighted when I felt thee leap in my womb. Elisabeth perceived thee also, just as thou didst promise me, and thou didst not deceive me, in making perfect in me thy lofty promise. Now I may see thee, sovereign rose, truly God and truly man. I honor thee as my gentle Babe, my true God and my Father.
Joseph:	Honor and magnificence, power, praise and reverence be thine, newborn King, Son of great Providence! May wisdom and all good things be given to thee. Thou art both a fine male Child and a high crowned King. On this high occasion embellished with joy, wherein daybreak comes early, thou hast led us to divine Providence.
Our Lady:	I thank thee, dreaded Power. I thank thee, divine King, who has accepted thy handmaiden so that I gave birth gently to thy son. Precious issue of Deity, humility brings thee from Heaven to become brother to humanity. In this pitiful place thou hast a spotless birth, Son of high degree born of a humble mother. What more can I do? I announce thee in a clear voice, my gentle Babe, my true God and my Father.
Joseph:	*Ave*, very precious fruit! *Ave*, gracious Savior! If I knew how to say more, I would say it with a humble and loving heart. This God knows. Now may God grant that I see thee in glory.
Our Lady:	May God provide for us through his grace. Joseph, there are such poor provisions in this shed that it is a great pity.
Joseph:	Here are six or seven swaddling clothes, such as I have been able to find. Wrap the Babe in them without grieving. He will make do well enough. I also brought some milk that I am

| | going to warm without delay, to provide him with a little nourishment. |
| *Our Lady:* | Very dear sire, may God reward you for going to such pains. |

Scene 23. The Annunciation to the Shepherds

Gabriel:	I am going to fulfill God's command concerning the Shepherds who are keeping watch tonight over their flocks. I will bring them the joyous news.
Michael:	You have beautiful company to help you.
Raphael:	I wish to travel that way with you to celebrate.

Here Gabriel goes away in front with great light toward the Shepherds and the others come very beautifully after. (G) Then Gabriel goes away toward the Shepherds with light. (M)

Aloris:	Oh God of Israel! What thing is that before and behind us? Never have I seen such light! Shepherds, look at that!
Ysambert:	Divine Virtue! What is that? Who ever saw such a marvel?
Pellion:	One would have to be mad not to marvel at seeing such light at midnight.
Rifflart:	I believe that the world is ending or that the moon has changed its course.
Aloris:	Ah, sweet God, give us help! That brightness astonishes us so much that we dare not move.
Gabriel:	Fear not: for, behold, I bring you good tidings of great joy, which shall be to all people. For unto you is born this day in the city of David a Saviour, which is Christ the Lord. And this shall be a sign unto you; Ye shall find the Babe wrapped in swaddling clothes, lying in a manger.
Raphael:	Come, Angels, with joyous pleasure let us commence a song about this mystery to rejoice the Shepherds.

They sing all together; Gloria in excelsis Deo et in terra pax hominibus bonae voluntatis! (G)

Michael:	Glory to God in the highest—
Uriel:	And on earth peace, good will toward men.4

Here the Angels return into Heaven, and one of them must always remain with Our Lady. (G)

Scene 24. The Shepherds

Aloris:	Oh Creator of all persons, here is news of high worth. We are so overwhelmed with joy that we do not know what we should do.
Ysambert:	If you would like to follow my advice, let us go into Bethlehem so that we may see this holy Babe. The visit will be hardly any trouble for us.
Pellion:	Ysambert, you have spoken wisely. Let each of us dress for the occasion. Let whoever wishes to go follow our footsteps.
Rifflart:	I will be among the first to go.
Aloris:	Our sheep will stay here. Garnier and Gombault will have the task of watching over them for a while until we return. Now are we well groomed? Does each man have everything he needs? Shall we depart?
Pellion:	Whenever you wish. Let's set forth, and may God guide us!

Scene 25. The Holy Family

Our Lady:	Oh my dear Son, I see thee lodged too simply, when I must bed thee in the manger for cattle. Thy poverty touches my heart, and yet I cannot improve thy situation.
Joseph:	I cannot restrain myself so that, in an abundance of pity, I dissolve in tears over this, when the King of Angels on high is born in such a humble place.
Our Lady:	May God's will be done.

Music. (G)

4. Luke 2:10–14.

Scene 26. The Three Kings

Here warn those who work the secret of the star to begin to show it.   (M)

Jaspar, First King:

In my heart I cannot ponder too often what this star signifies that I see beneath the circle of the moon. This is not a common star, for the others of common course shine by night, not at all by day, and this star shines at all hours. Concerning its location, it is not like the others, for it is marvelously much lower to the horizon, and the others are on high. I must conclude that this star is a sign to us of some lofty and admirable mystery that has just taken place.

Anthiocus, Knight:

Lord King, you have judged prudently. To reinforce your conclusion, this star cannot be a comet, for whenever a comet appears and remains in the sky, it shows light plainly by night, but by day it does not shed any light. We must conclude that this star is of another nature as a sign of some mystery.

Jaspar:

This is a true and perfect star, as clear as Venus. I believe that the days have been accomplished for the star that Balaam greatly prized, who prophesied: there shall come a Star out of Jacob, and a Sceptre shall rise out of Israel.[5]

Celsander, Knight:

Never have I seen a star shine with such admirable light, so I agree with you, Lord King. May the One be born of whom the prophets have written.

Jaspar:

If it were so, by word or by Scripture, that I might know the truth about the mystery of the Nativity of the Child promised so long ago who must be King of the Jews, never would I remain here until I had adored him in just and true obedience, for since the time of my own childhood I have vowed this. I do

---

5. Numbers 24:17; Isaiah 7:14.

not know whether he is born or not, where he is, or what his name is. But if it is possible, I will travel until I find him, no matter which way I must turn.

Anthiocus: Sire, if it pleases you to depart, all necessary things are ready.

Signal Melchior that he must be ready to speak after Jaspar.   (M)

Jaspar: God will lead us, and so will the good King whom we search! Here is how we will manage so that, with great effort, we may arrive at our destination. The star appears in the east in order to guide us somehow. We will travel along beneath it without deviating from our path.

Here they set out on their journey following the star.   (G)

Melchior, Second King:

What does this star signify that is so low to the horizon? It appears to outshine the others. I assure you, it must mean that the high crowned King of the Jews is born at this very hour. There I see the unerring sign.

Cadoras, Knight: Lord King, take care what you say, for it is not a petty matter to foretell such a mystery. It is a good idea to doubt for a while, in order to have greater certitude later.

Melchior: My words are good and virtuous, and are based on the teachings of Balaam, who saw in a vision what he described in a parable. There shall come a Star out of Jacob, by which it is meant that a Virgin will be born and will bear such a great King that he will hold all Israel in his dominion. His coming was promised a long time ago by the entire law of Moses. Prophets sing of hardly anything else in text and commentary. When I saw this star in its unique course with its unique light, I judged that this star announced the Nativity of that same King to us. I say that he must have been born today when the star made its appearance.

Polidorus, Knight: Lord King, your reasoning is very well presented and proceeds from very sound logic. But if the birth of this King is ordained, what do you wish to conclude regarding our own participation in this mystery?

Melchior: I will set forth on a voyage and I will forever continue traveling until I have offered this King honor and homage, and I will carry a large part of my treasure to him.

Cadoras: If you wish to depart, our provisions are ready.

Melchior: May the dreaded Virtue of God be with us!

Here they set out on their way like the others and walk along after. (G)

Balthazar, Third King:
Now may God be praised, for I see the clear and beautiful star! I have waited for a long time with great desire for this coming, hoping that the promise made long ago by Balaam might be fulfilled. Now I praise the God of nature for this star with my heart and mind.

Lucanus, Knight: What personal gain have you thought of in this matter, noble King? You prize this star and grant it high authority, but I do not know how this star profits you.

Balthazar: Lucanus, the nobility of this celestial sign is no petty matter. This star indicates to us that, according to several documents that our predecessors have given us, the high natural King of the Jews has been born in the mortal world. The documents all attest that this King is both God and man. Never will I be at ease until I have seen the Babe and have provided him with my treasure, while adoring his high nobility.

Pirodes, Knight You speak excellently, noble King, and it is appropriate that such a virtuous King should be honored by our great efforts. But the difficulty lies in finding him, for no news reaches us concerning his royal court.

Balthazar: This star is moving along rather low to the horizon and it is headed toward Judaea. We will keep sight of the star and fol-

low it. Now I pray to God from whom all good comes that
this journey will lead us to joy.

Music.   (G)

Scene 27. The Adoration of the Shepherds

Then the Shepherds walk and, going along, Aloris speaks.   (M)

Aloris:	Shepherds, I realize that we have not yet decided what gifts to bring to this little Babe.
Pellion:	I have already thought what worthy gift I will take to the Babe.
Rifflart:	What gift?
Pellion:	Now make some silly guesses.
Rifflart:	Your Shepherd's crook?
Pellion:	No. My Shepherd's crook is too essential; without it I can do nothing. Even if the Babe desired it, I doubt that he should have it.
Rifflart:	Will you give him your dog?
Pellion:	Certainly not. Who would bring back my sheep?
Rifflart:	Then what will you give him? Is it so pretty and elegant a gift?
Pellion:	I will give him my new flageolet. He could not refuse it. The last time I was in Bethlehem, I went to a small shop and bought it for two pennies. That was a real bargain, for I do not know any man who could have bought it for four pennies. But even if it had cost more, the Babe would have it.
Aloris:	Your gift is generous.
Ysambert:	I will give him a rattle, marvelously well made, which will say "click click" in his ear. At least when the Babe cries, the rattle will appease him, and he will be quiet for a while.
Aloris:	I have a beautiful wooden calendar to teach him the days and the months. With this calendar the Babe will learn all the feast

The Adoration of the Shepherds

days, including Lent. I think this is the perfect gift. Each saint
has his own little illustration under which his name is written
in large letters. That will give the Babe an advantage, for at
least when he is older, he will learn his alphabet.

Rifflart: That's a gift fit to be given to a count. As for me, I am giving
the Babe a little bell that has been hanging on the tip of my
headdress for a long time, and a very fine top that is in my
satchel. There is neither Shepherd nor Shepherdess in the
world who can find a gift of greater novelty.

In saying this, they must enter Bethlehem. (M)

Pellion: Now we are in the city of Bethlehem, thanks be to God. We
need only look for the place where the Infant and the mother
are.

Ysambert: Let's look carefully. The Angels have given us a sign that will
tell us when we have found the right place. I hope we find it.

Aloris: My heart tells me that this is the place. Let us take a chance
and enter.

Rifflart: I agree; this must be the place.

Pellion: Now let us all kneel humbly and worship the gentle and precious Babe, for I know in my heart that he is both God and
man.

Ysambert: I believe that he is the very gentle Emmanuel, the Saviour of
Israel. I would like to present to him a song, such as I know
how, loyally and simply.

Child of high nobility, well art thou born!
Child of high nobility,
By sorrow and true humility well seasoned,
In thee is all wisdom, all honor, all generosity.
All good is given to thee!
Thou art ordained to relieve our frailties;
Thus, adored Son, sweet and tender youth,
Well art thou born!

Aloris: In simplicity of understanding,
We render homage to thee.
In simplicity of understanding,
Dear Infant, we come to see thee
With joyous courage, to perform our duty,
To obtain thy benevolence for help in our lives.
Our simple greetings please receive with goodwill,
Powerful and wise King.
With body and soul and all we have,
We render homage to thee!

Pellion: Thou art King of the whole world,
And such do we believe thee to be.
Thou art King of the whole world:
Our hope relies on thee, wherever we may be.
Worldly sin corresponds to this impure place
In which we see thee.
We magnify thee with praises in simple words,
And we confide to thee that in thee
All grace is abundant,
And such do we believe thee to be!

Rifflart: Oh high Nativity! Oh very noble Infant!
Oh high Nativity to which thou hast invited us!
True triumphant God, when I see thee lying
In such great humility, my heart breaks!
My body and soul sense that thou art true Deity
Who descends for our sake to adopt our humanity.
Oh very noble Infant!

Here Our Lady takes the Child and sits, then puts him on her lap, and the Shepherds adore him, each one offering his gift. (G)

Ysambert: Let each of us give thee a gift, gentle little Babe. Receive them with pure goodwill, for we have no other gifts.

Aloris: Lady, we thank you for your sweetness and mercy to us in the presence of your Son whom you love so much.

Pellion: We will consider ourselves blessed for as long as we are able to live in this world.

Our Lady: Brothers, I pray that God will give you the perfection of your desires. I know that the divine pleasure has been to reveal this mystery to you, for which reason I neither can nor wish to conceal the Babe.

Rifflart: Oh Son of highest authority, Master of all earthly kingdoms, I sense thy love so strongly that it grieves me to leave thee.

Ysambert: Yet we must think about returning to guard our flocks. Farewell, gentle and tender Infant.

Pellion: Farewell, Infant of noble birth.

Ysambert: Farewell, mind that understands everything.

Aloris: Farewell, treasure of God.

Rifflart: Farewell, very humble humanity.

Pellion: Farewell, very lofty Divinity. We adore thee at our leave-taking.

Joseph: May the One whom the human heart cannot comprehend be your escort, my children.

Here the Shepherds return.   (G)

Our Lady: Oh my dear Son, when I hold thee my heart leaps with joy, nor would I ever have enough of kissing thy sweet face. I cannot make thee comfortable now in this too unfavorable place; it weighs on my heart. Now let the milk of my breasts suffice for thee, for as long as there may be a drop of milk, thou shalt not be refused.

Joseph: If God pleases, I think that there will be so much milk that there will be no lack.

Scene 28. The Rejoicing of the Shepherds

Aloris: We have seen a noble mystery. May the power of God be praised, honored, and magnified, when through his glorious messengers he has chosen to make us Shepherds wise, first in all the nation, concerning such a noble Incarnation.

Ysambert: The angelic Annunciation was made manifest and true.

Garnier, Fifth Shepherd:
Why do those men who are coming directly this way have such joyous faces? Gombault, fine sir, look a little at the way they are behaving.

Gombault, Sixth Shepherd:
Certainly I do not know who they are, but they are coming this way very joyfully. They are looking up at the sky so much that it is a great marvel. Who are they?

Garnier: I am astonished. We must watch them. Would those not be our companions returning from Bethlehem?

Gombault: Now that I have studied their behavior, I believe that those are the very men.

Garnier: I recognize them. See there—Pellion and Rifflart, Aloris and Ysambert. At least those are their Shepherds' crooks.

Gombault: Greetings, gentle Shepherds. Give us the news right away; tell us all.

Pellion: The loftiest news that ever was, and have no suspicions about it. For certain, we announce to you the birth of the Lord of the whole world and true Saviour, who has come to save us.

Garnier: Is this true?

Rifflart: We have seen him and adored his person, and we believe he is the true God who made everything.

Gombault: Is this the Christ promised by the prophets?

Aloris: This is the Christ whom God the Father has sent. The Angels bore witness to him in announcing the mystery to us. They sent us to Bethlehem, and we departed according to their word. When we arrived in those parts, we found the King of glory, born in a humble shed, lying in a manger, and the mother on her knees before him and adoring him.

Ysambert:	God's charitable humility leads him to this birth.
Garnier:	Here is marvelous news and of very great significance!
Gombault:	Here is marvelous news: the Son of God is born!
Pellion:	Valiant Shepherds, let each of us return to guard his flocks with care, and let us serve God with devotion and simplicity.

Music. (G)

THE PLAY OF THE THREE KINGS

Scene 29. The Journey of the Three Kings

Anthiocus: Lord King, if it pleases the infinite Power, may you rejoice and make merry. We have found company traveling along our route.

They go along little by little. (M)

Jaspar: May the divine King be praised. Our voyage will be all the more joyous and worthwhile. Those seem to be persons of noble array.

Celsander: I believe that is a powerful King who wishes to travel our way. If it would please you to speak with him, you will know his intention.

Jaspar: Here we will pause, ever awaiting their arrival. Lord King, may the one God, governing Heaven and the skies, keep you in his grace!

Melchior: And may the one God who governs the skies maintain and perfect you in honor and power due to you!

Jaspar: If you are going the same way and wish for us to travel together for a while, we would be delighted to accompany you.

Melchior: Lord King, to judge by your appearance and considering the path you are traveling, we have the same objective.

Jaspar: Where are you going?

Melchior: We do not know into what land we travel, but this star gives us a sign that the new King of the Jews is born. Thus I am traveling along, following this star, to adore him and render him homage.

Jaspar: In my heart I have longed to undertake a voyage similar to yours, so my men and I have felt impelled to travel there hastily.

Melchior: May God be highly praised because we have met so appropriately. If you please, my men and I will accompany you there. I hope that we will find news to gladden us, for the star, our guide, advances ahead of us.

Jaspar: I hope that it will lead us as far as the place where that noble King is born. Now let us travel rapidly.

They go together. (M)

Cadoras: My lords, be not in haste. I see another company of people who are following us.

Polidorus: Perhaps that is also a great lord who wishes to travel our way.

Balthazar: Noble lords, may God give you whatever your hearts desire! Where go my worthy lords?

Jaspar: Lord King, we follow this star that guides us, at the will of God and with his aid. May God permit this star to lead us to a good destination.

Balthazar: My thought is very near to yours, loyal Kings. Soon it will be ten days since this star first made its appearance to us in my region. In my heart I understood that the King of Heaven is born to the Virgin. I have come into this land by constantly following this star, hoping that it will guide me to the sacred place where this mystery has been accomplished.

Melchior: When we noticed the star, we departed from Araby and Sabba. We too are led by this star, and as long as we see it, never do we cease traveling, because we sense that it will stop in some faraway province. We anticipate with certainty that in the place where this star halts, there will be the mansion of the Virgin who is mother to the newborn King.

Balthazar: You will offer me the greatest courtesy and advantage, Kings of noble bearing, if you please to admit me to your company.

Jaspar: We rejoice in the encouragement of your royal company, and were it as far as to Constantinople, we would loyally accompany you.

Lucanus: Let whoever believes my words make haste to set forth again, for the star is moving ahead constantly. We are not at leisure to remain here.

King Herod and the Three Kings

Pirodes:	As long as we choose to follow this star, we need have no fear of losing our way.
Jaspar:	I pray that God will guard us from harm and hindrance.

Music. (G) *Take care that the star be hidden when the Three Kings are near Jerusalem. (M)*

Balthazar:	I do not know how to determine in what land we have arrived.
Melchior:	Never during the whole journey have I been so amazed as I am now. The star, which was shining and guiding us, has suddenly failed us.
Jaspar:	I do not know where our star has gone, but our eyes see nothing. If God does not give us help, we are in a precarious situation.
Balthazar:	God will give us comfort. One suggestion is to ask what place we have come to at this hour.
Anthiocus:	Lord Kings, I assure you that our company is at present in Judaea. And so that this may be perceived as truth, that is the city of Jerusalem that we see before us.
Jaspar:	Anthiocus, are you entirely certain?
Anthiocus:	Sire, I reply that it is so. I have been acquainted with this region for a long time.
Jaspar:	Lord Kings, since it is thus, that the star has left us, and since we are near enough to the city ahead of us, let whosoever believes my words enter the city. Let us go seek the local sages to have their counsel regarding the mystery.
Melchior:	We will all accompany you and be guided by your wisdom.
Balthazar:	Since we are in the city, we may now inquire whether there is news anywhere in the region about the newborn King.

Scene 30. The Naming of Jesus

Eliachin:	God the Father be praised. The Babe has been very gently circumcised. Mary, you are the mother. Take care what name the Child will have.

Our Lady:	No change will be made from the name highly assigned that was predestined for him. As soon as the Angel announced his birth to me, he proclaimed the name to me. I do not wish to add anything to it.
Eliachin:	What was that name?
Our Lady	Jesus.
Eliachin:	Jesus is a name of great value and is a worthy name for our Saviour. Now may God grant that Jesus will save us so well that he will receive us in glory.
Joseph:	So truly do I believe it that I have perfect faith in him.

Scene 31. The Jewish Elders

Jaspar:	Lords of notable prudence, Where is the place full of grace Where the high King of the Jews, Newborn, has his residence?
Melchior:	We ask to be in his presence To honor this newborn Sovereign. Lords of notable prudence, Where is the place full of grace?
Balthazar:	His star of great power We have chosen for certain In the Orient, for we arrive Suddenly to see his magnificence.
Anthiocus:	Lords of notable prudence, Where is the place full of grace Where the high King of the Jews, Newborn, has his residence?[6]

Gamaliel, Scribe of the Law:

Here is a marvelous eloquence that causes great suspicion. Lords, you are asking a question that must not be answered

6. Matthew 2:2.

with frivolity, but with great danger. You are inquiring about the new King of the Jews! You shall not know anything about him from us, for we agree that there is no news about him here. Therefore, we do not know how to respond.

Roboan, Second Scribe:

At present we have no King of our own lineage, so the land is governed by a foreigner who proclaims himself King of the Jews. For at sword point he usurped the land, and he holds it as a vassal of the Emperor of Rome, who is lord of the whole world. The King is named Herod; he maintains us in his love as well as he can, so we do not rebel against him. I do not know if he is so renowned that his fame has reached the places from which you came. We will gladly take you to him.

Jaspar:

He is not at all the One whom we are seeking. Nevertheless, it would be prudent for us to hear his reasoning, to see whether he knows anything about the Nativity.

Zorobabel, Pharisee:

If there is news, I suppose that King Herod will have heard it. Now follow me; I am going to him to announce your arrival.

Music. (G)

Scene 32. The Audience with King Herod

Zorobabel:

Lord King, may your nobility be maintained in strength and honor.

Herod, King of Judaea:

May the God of Israel grant the wealth that your heart desires. What news do you bring, Zorobabel? How are our citizens doing? Are the scribes and Pharisees at peace? Do they need anything?

Zorobabel:

Sire, I only know that all goes well. I have brought before you three noteworthy crowned Kings, who desire and propose to speak only two words to your royal majesty.

King Herod and the Three Kings

Herod:	It seems to me that this news is special and strange. What is this? Have these three Kings come here together now to me?
Zorobabel:	Yes, from diverse kingdoms: from Araby, Sabba, and Tharse.
Herod:	Since their journey is so long, they must have come for a matter of great consequence. Do you know what they have come to ask for? You have permission to reveal it.
Zorobabel:	Sire, you will hear them speak, and you will hear what they tell you.
Herod:	We will give them audience.
Jaspar:	Noble King filled with wisdom, may he who contains all power within himself increase your honor, and may he give you abundant treasures.
Herod:	Noble Kings full of prowess, may your high and noble renown never fall into oblivion. Thus may Mohammed, my infinite god in his highness, maintain your valor. Would you please be seated here, and afterward, we will talk.
Melchior:	We will gladly obey your wishes.

They are seated. *(M)*

Herod:	Now then, lords, you may speak frankly from your hearts of the cause that moves you, even though we realize that your words might bring us to grief.
Jaspar:	Lord King, to briefly explain our purpose, it is true that not long ago, God manifested a star to us. It follows a course completely different from that of other stars. When we heeded its clear and obvious mystery, we remembered what the prophet Balaam promised us, who said that a beautiful star will appear when the high Christ is incarnated to reign over the Jews. The prophet has shown us the meaning of the sign: that the King is born. The star was shown throughout our countries. That is the cause that leads us to seek his high Majesty and to present some gifts to him.

Herod:	Worthy lords, let us wait a little. You are prudent and wise men. Do not offer such language if you do not mean it sincerely, for it would affect our majesty greatly if what you say were to come to pass.
Melchior:	As for what Balaam prophesied, we know of its certainty and truth. Here is how: the star that he prophesied does not have a circular movement like those in the heavens, but it travels in a straight line. We have really been able to see it moving along in front of us. It has led us here without deviating, thanks be to God; as soon as the city was in sight, the star subtly faded away, which makes us all the more certain.
Herod:	Counts, knights, and lords, listen to this devilish talk here that touches greatly upon our dominion! Lords, take care what you relate. Do you ignore our power, our throne, our law? Do you ignore that we are the true King of Judaea and of all men in this kingdom? Where do you think you are going? What Prince, what King are you seeking? Is there any other King today but us? Is there any man from across the seas so bold that he dares to proclaim himself King of the Jews? Let him come for combat! We will combat him with so much force that he will be well entertained.
Adracus, Count:	Who is so bold that he will say that any King governs us other than our King Herod, may God increase his honor?
Hermogenes, a Knight to King Herod:	
	We have no other governor, no other King, no other captain than Herod. That is a certain thing, for we obey only him.
Arphazac, Second Knight:	
	There is no man whom we would not destroy if he wished to say the contrary.
Adracus:	One cannot make me angrier nor trouble my mind more than by impeding and distressing our King in his noble reign.
Herod:	Who doubts that I will always reign? I will do battle against everyone!

Balthazar:	Lord King, be not enraged. Although we wish to find the newborn King, we do not wish to grieve any soul, nor you, nor your royalty. We search for the truth as men far away from their native countries.
Herod:	What? Are you astonished to hear such words from our mouth? Does it not seem to you that this matter pertains to us? We feel ourselves very strongly affected by it, and we want to impress on you that the kingdom is in our hands. And we do not know any sovereign over us except the Emperor of Rome, who is our true lord; we do not contradict him. And to inform you of the facts, this country has wished to rebel for a long time against the Emperor and his representatives. Now we have reduced and conquered this country by force, for which reason the Emperor has given us its crown. Thus we do not dread anyone who, by himself or with allies, tries to overthrow us in some wicked war.
Jaspar:	We do not wish to contradict you, sire, but this much we do believe: that this King whom we seek is greater and stronger than you.
Herod:	We are not opposed to that. If he has lands and a great country, as long as he is not King of the Jews, his reign does not affect ours in any way.
Jaspar:	He is and will be King of the Jews, and what is more, King of this whole beautiful world. He must govern everywhere as Judge and Reformer.
Herod:	Lords, listen: what horror, what pestilence, what madness, what rage! This is the wickedest, the most arrogant, the most displeasing language that ever was! I feel burning grief to hear such terrible reasoning.
Arphazac:	Lord King, we are silent, for we do not accept their faith, and we maintain that there is no King over Jewry but you.
Herod:	Shall we lose lordship that has cost us so dearly? Shall we lose royalty of which our valor is worthy? Shall we lose dominion, sold to us with such harsh punishment? Oh Fortune, there is

nothing in thee. Fortune, marvelous beast: thou and thy detestable wheel! Let us spin the wheel of Fortune and let it do its bloody worst!

Gamaliel: Sire, you must not demonstrate such mourning over this matter.

Herod: All joy has fled from me since someone is challenging me, for a thing that was conquered with great effort must be more dearly guarded.

Gamaliel: That is true, but let us restore peace between yourself and these noteworthy lords who bring you several reasons why they have come to adore this King. I do not believe that they are insisting that there exists any mortal man in any empire who can call himself King of the Jews other than you. Have no doubts. But there is one point about which I wonder. This King of whom they tell us, and about whom they make such lofty speeches, might be the newborn Christ, who the prophets have plainly affirmed must come. That is why these Kings have arrived, it seems, for their Scriptures tell them that the Christ must govern the whole world. For when he comes, he will maintain his reign in peace and he will be the true King of Israel.

Herod: You speak clearly, Gamaliel, and you draw our attention to a matter about which we were not thinking, since it touches upon this Christ. He must be of as great virtue as you Jews believe him to be, as you learn about him in your Scriptures. Every man knows of his renown well enough, but to know whether or not he is born, there lies the dilemma and the danger.

Roboan: We cannot judge this. You have heard what these notable Kings have related; they are certain that he is born. We do not know if this is true.

Herod: What they say is not to be believed, even if everyone accepts it. First, if the Christ were indeed born, we believe that the Jews would have known of it. His birth would have been celebrated with such great solemnities that there never would have been such great rejoicing. Now there is no news of such a birth, and no such festivities are evident to us. As for the star that they tell us has been shown to them, it is an illusion of the first order, a fantasy, a dream, a hope, a great lie to whoever pauses and believes in it. And when a real star appears, does it not follow that a man may only guess what mystery it signifies in his own life?

Gamaliel: Truly, unless there is revelation from God.

Herod: The Kings are not speaking of divine revelation. Their argument is based on the illusion that the star signifies that the Christ must have come.

Adracus: Such reasoning arrives at no conclusion. It is illogical to base such a great mystery on such a very small appearance.

Herod: Since it may be of consequence, we would very much like to know in what place or territory the Christ is prophesied to be born. Since he must be your master, lord Jews, it is reasonable to suppose that you know something about this, for which reason you may speak all the better about it.

Gamaliel: Lord King, to reply to you, it is true and we wish to maintain that the Christ must come. But if he has already appeared, he has not appeared to us at all, nor is there any news, so we speak to you no more about it.

Zorobabel: But as for the place and the prophecy about where the Christ must be born, the wise men who study the prophets carefully say that it is appropriate to search for him in Bethlehem, in the noble land of Judaea. The good prophet Micah prophesied about him thus: "But thou, Bethlehem Ephratah, though thou be little among the thousands of Judah, yet out of thee shall he come forth unto me that is to be ruler in Israel; whose goings forth have been from of old, of everlasting."[7] That is what the prophet sings.

Herod: The song is not insignificant, but of very great authority.

7. Micah 5:2.

Roboan:	Zorobabel has accurately quoted the Scripture that speaks of this matter, and it explains in full the reasoning on which we base our beliefs.
Zorobabel:	In all the Scriptures we find neither authority nor clear teaching that so obviously assigns the place where the Saviour must be born.
Roboan:	We all believe that this must be in Bethlehem, as Micah has said.
Herod:	We heed the prophet's word, and it is easily believable. Please do not be displeased if we wish to retreat a little while to speak two or three words in private to these notable Kings. We will return soon enough.
Gamaliel:	Lord King and sovereign master, do all that pleases you.
Hermogenes:	Noble Kings, you must follow King Herod, who is departing from hence. He wishes to speak in private with you, from what I have understood.
Jaspar:	Well then, arise, let us not keep him waiting. Let us go and hear his discourse.
Herod:	Noble Kings, now that by good counsel we are here in private, is it certain and proven that you have seen this star, and that it has appeared to you in the manner that you describe?
Jaspar:	Lord King, never doubt that it is true about the star.
Herod:	Truly. But perhaps the star was of the same nature and movement as other stars in the heavens, for you hardly remark on any difference.
Melchior:	Sire, begging your reverence's pardon and speaking by the letter, I can name three great differences. First, those stars that are in the heavens have a circular path of motion. This one did not turn in a circle, but it preceded us in a straight line. Second, everyone perceives that, no matter what star is being observed, although the sky does turn and move slowly, we do not see that star moving because of its high and great distance from the horizon. We have been able to see this star moving so very clearly that we have based our journey solely on the star's

path of movement. Third, no man sees the stars shine by day, for the sun outshines stars with its bright light and renders their light impotent to be seen in the sun's presence. Well, this star's light was shown to us in the brightest part of the day so very plainly that all of us saw it. Thus I say that the star signified that some great mystery has taken place.

Herod: You have sustained your theory well and have proved it with logic. But speak to us about the exact season when you saw it.

Balthazar: It was ten days ago or nearly so when the star first appeared, and it stayed with us so consistently that we have been able to reach Jerusalem at a leisurely pace by following the star. So we decided to come here.

Herod: Are you sure there is no more? For this matter touches us, to tell the truth.

Jaspar: There is neither more nor less, sire. By our faith we affirm this to you.

Take care that those working the secret of the star make this star appear, as soon as Melchior takes leave of Herod. (M)

Herod: Lord Kings, I believe you utterly and I consider you to be very credible; a more convincing argument and more noteworthy persons of honor cannot be found. And to make our will known, we are overjoyed about this noble event and about this newborn King; this pleases us beautifully. Since if he is the Christ, we realize that we owe him true homage, here is what you will do. You will go to Bethlehem to diligently inquire about the Infant, about his birth, about his parents, and principally, about his residence. And when you have found him, in that very hour return here to us so that we and all our men may go to render him homage, and honor him with glad hearts as we ought to do.

Melchior: Lord King, once we have gone there, if we may know the truth, be certain that we will do our duty to you so that you will be satisfied. Farewell, sire.

The star is shown.   (M)

Herod:	Farewell, my lords, and may God guide you.

Scene 33. The Star of Bethlehem

Then the Three Kings go along and, when they are outside Bethlehem, Balthazar speaks.   (M)

Balthazar:	I perceive our star shining! It seems to me that it has returned.
Jaspar:	Ah, blessed be the star, and praised be God a thousand times!
Melchior:	I see it truly. It has the form, the brightness, the path, the height, and the beauty. Praised be God for his merciful heart!
Anthiocus:	Never have I been so joyful as in seeing it again.
Lucanus:	This is the most beautiful gift for us that we might ever possess.
Celsander:	This is no time to stop; let us travel on with a joyous will.
Pirodes:	We need no other guide to conduct our voyage.
Polidorus:	Now may God grant that through his guidance our masters may reach the place where all their desire is, so truly that they may have certitude!
Cadoras:	This star has great meaning. May God grant that this sign may give medicine to our souls.

Music.   (G)

Scene 34. The Court of King Herod

Herod:	Lords and princes of the law, you have been vigilant for our welfare; all your good efforts will be rewarded. Go home whenever you please, as this matter has been swiftly settled.
Roboan:	Lord King, we take our leave of you.
Gamaliel:	If you need anything from us on any day, do not spare our labor.

Zorobabel: We are swiftly yours to serve you with good and cordial love.

Here they each go to their place.   (G)

Scene 35. The Adoration of the Three Kings

Anthiocus: Lords, you have traveled so far that your journey will soon be over. I see that this star pauses and only shows itself over one place, now that we have entered the city of Bethlehem.

They enter Bethlehem.   (M)

Jaspar: I necessarily conclude that we will find the high King whom we seek in this place, since the star has paused here.

Melchior: Now we are beyond our grief and delivered of great doubt, as we have clear proof of our mystery by two means. The scribes and Pharisees related to us that it is said by the prophet that the high Christ must be born here, and the star indicates this also, which gives us double doctrine.

Celsander: May the high divine Power be worthily praised.

Balthazar: We must look above what habitation the star is stationed now, for if we choose the place, we shall have all our desire.

Pirodes: My lord, it appears to me, according to where the star is fixed, that it is this little shed, for the star is precisely above it.

Polidorus: We cannot go wrong if we enter and see, for God can make great mysteries appear in a small place.

Jaspar: First let us prepare our offerings, so that in adoring the Babe, each of us may offer his gift without causing delay. Let us each offer his gift in turn. Well then, King Melchior, what gift will you present?

Melchior: I will give the Babe gold, myrrh, and frankincense that smells very sweet, for it is the custom of our land. Such a gift must one give to such a King. And you, King Balthazar?

The Adoration of the Three Kings

Balthazar:	The same. King Jaspar, are your gifts different from ours?
Jaspar:	Not at all; they are like yours. Whoever carefully thinks about our gifts will realize that they are of great significance. With frankincense we manifest the Babe to be true God, and such do we confess him to be; with gold we show him to be King; and with myrrh, he is also mortal man. These are three gifts of great value.
Cadoras:	Lord Kings, the gifts are ready. Enter whenever you please.
Melchior:	Now enter first, King Jaspar; your rank merits it.
Balthazar:	That is as it should be, for you are the eldest.
Jaspar:	Noble Kings, by your leave; you accord me too great honor. Look, worthy lords, at the humility, the patience of the powerful Magnificence! He humbles himself so that his gentle and tender Infancy is entrusted to the donkeys and the oxen.
Melchior:	Let us kneel and offer our gifts.

Then they all kneel. *(M)*

Jaspar:	I hail thee, God of glorious Heaven, immortal God, God virtuous over all, true Son of God who dost create Heaven and earth. I hail thee, only Monarch of the world, whom human heart cannot comprehend. I understand that thou hast taken our human form from the body of the pure Virgin, in order to redeem thine innocent friends. I give thee gifts of gold, myrrh, and frankincense, showing thee to be King, God, and mortal man.
Melchior:	I hail thee, dear gracious Infant, very noble Son, very holy precious fruit, the choice of the most Beautiful. I hail thee, most delightful of the gentle, most benign of the merciful, celestial bread, true cornerstone. Perfect love leads me to thee, recognizing thy high power. Thou dost condescend to deliver humanity, and if I have no fine enough gifts for thee, pardon thy serf. I give thee gifts of gold, myrrh, and frankincense, showing thee to be King, God, and mortal man.

Balthazar: I hail thee, King of abundant Heaven, fruit of salvation, happiest of riches, treasure to whom none can compare. Now if thou art naked and poor in worldly goods, thou has so much within thyself that none can comprehend. For thou hast descended from highest Heaven to life on earth as Judge and Regent of the quick and the dead. I give thee gifts of gold, myrrh, and frankincense, showing thee to be King, God, and mortal man.

Here Our Lady holds the Infant on her lap and each of the Three Kings presents his gift in turn.   (G)

Our Lady: Noble lords, you are presenting a great sum of goods to my dear Son, Jesus. But you are poorly received, which weighs on my heart, for I cannot do better for you. You see this rude abode, which is unsuitable for entertaining such noble Kings. You see the poor little Babe in these swaddling clothes. You see his poor friends and his poor mother who watches over him.

Jaspar: His poor estate does not disturb us, dear lady, I promise you. But the time will never come when we will cease to feel blessed because we have seen your Child. We believe that he knows all and can do all, as the true Son of God the Father.

Melchior: Lady, very venerable mother, may you watch over him with joy. So pleasant is he to behold that no heart can comprehend him.

Balthazar: My noble lady, we take our leave of you.
We greet you humbly.

Our Lady: I pray to the King of Heaven
That he may repay your good deeds!

Joseph: Lords, you have witnessed our humble household;
We live simply here.
Since you wish to head homeward,
May God keep you from harm!

Jaspar:	Good man, think carefully About this sacred, precious Child: See that he lacks nothing For his sweet upbringing.
Melchior:	My noble lady, we take our leave of you. We greet you humbly.
Our Lady:	I pray to the King of Heaven That he may repay your good deeds!

They depart. *(M)*

Scene 36. The Inn in Bethlehem

Balthazar:	Worthy lords, we must find lodgings for tonight.
Anthiocus:	If you would follow me a few steps, I have found entirely favorable lodgings in a spacious inn where you will be very comfortable.
Melchior:	Sire, please enter; you are our eldest.

They enter. *(M)*

Eleazar, Innkeeper:	
	Lord Kings, your chamber is already reserved. I have prepared your beds and your private chapel, and I have made such preparations as befit your estate. If you would like for me to bring you a fine platter of fresh meats and some good wine, you shall have your fill.
Lucanus:	You have spoken like an elegant host. In brief, our lords do not wish to eat or drink; they only desire rest.
Celsander:	This does not suit me at all, for I see neither feast nor entertainment here. I do not want to go without a meal.
Eleazar:	You have spoken like a lord. No amount of rest is worth it; I shall look for some food for you, as long as you can pay for it. Let your masters remain in peaceful seclusion here.

Then the Innkeeper goes to look for something to eat and drink. (M)

Polidorus: Now let us diligently attend to our dinner.

Cadoras: At the court of a King, fine friends, it's each man for himself. Whoever does not act thus is unwise.

Here the Three Kings drink once and then lie down on their beds. (M)

God the Father: Raphael, bear a message to the three wise and discreet Kings; go to them and tell them that they must not return to Herod. They must turn their path toward the sea to return home into their regions, for the evil King intends to kill the Babe, if he can.

Raphael: Triumphant Father, it will be accomplished this very hour.

Music. (G) Then Raphael goes. (M)

Raphael: Noble Kings, God the Father sends you news here through me, and very expressly commands you not to go to Herod. Turn your steps toward the sea and sail to your homelands. The tyrant wishes to ask you about Jesus, not to adore him, but to put him to death, if possible. Therefore, Kings of great valor, let all of you be on your guard.

Here Raphael returns. (G) Here he goes back into Heaven. (M)

Jaspar: Worthy lords, now let each of us beware of Herod and not return home by way of his palace. He is a felonious tyrant, as the Angel warns us.

Melchior: Arise, knights! Let each man prepare for the voyage; it is high time to depart. God has been pleased to warn us what we must do today.

Scene 37. The Homeward Journey of the Three Kings

Anthiocus: Our boat has abundant provisions. Arise, Sailor. Clothe your-self and hoist the sail.

The Sailor: Lords, step within. We have such a strong wind that we will sail to Tharse faster than a thunderbolt. Arrange yourselves carefully: one in the middle, one on each side.

Celsander: Sailor, raise the mast!

The Sailor: We have such a strong wind that no man could hope for better.

Balthazar: I pray that God will lead us homeward in joy and perfect rejoicing!

Scene 38. The Presentation of Jesus at the Temple

Saint Simeon, the Prophet:

Oh old age, rude estate of impotence and great feebleness! I have lived so long that I am weary of life. My youth has fled me, and I only await death's grip as a man nearly dead and de-prived of solace. Messiah, my God, when wilt thou come? Sweet Christ, when shall I see thee, alas? Immortal God, thou hast promised me that although death has overthrown and wearied me, my life will not end until I have seen the Christ, thy Son of nobility. Thou hast promised me, and I believe it, that I shall not be finished in this world or die in the flesh un-til I have seen him, and I hope that I shall embrace him whom I know to be my eternal life. And so, true God, if this is thy promise, I have perfect faith in it. Do not hide from me that which I hold so dear. I shall never cease to pray to you: good God, remember me, and may it please you that the day of hu-manity's Redemption shall come. Send consolation to the sons of Israel, your friends, as you have promised throughout the entire law of Moses.

Music. (G)

Eliachin:	We are more joyous than ever that we have come to the holy Temple. This is a sacred place wherein we may learn by example to follow the path of all virtues.
Joseph:	Let us each think of serving God with perfect devotion. Then we will present our offerings with a good heart and will.

Here they kneel. (G) Then they all kneel and, meanwhile, Simeon speaks. (M)

Simeon:	Lady, who of your own goodwill brings this little Babe, approach and present him at the altar very reverently.
Our Lady:	I will gladly accomplish it; such is surely my intention.

Then she places the offering on the altar, and their offerings are two turtledoves and two pigeons. (M)

Simeon:	To thee be adoration, praise, veneration, oh holy Virgin chosen among all. How much this worthy fruit of thy womb profits thee and all mankind! With hands joined in prayer, I ask that thy mercy may permit me to hold the Babe in my arms. I will end my days more easily.
Our Lady:	May the will of God always be done.

Then Simeon takes Jesus and holds him in his arms. (M)

Simeon:	*Nunc dimittis servum tuum.* Lord, now lettest thou thy servant depart in peace, according to thy word: For mine eyes have seen thy salvation, Which thou hast prepared before the face of all people; A light to lighten the Gentiles, and the glory of thy people Israel. Oh dear Child, what a hard journey thou shalt yet have to travel before the time comes when the Scriptures are accomplished through thy body! Very sweet Son, very gentle Jesus Christ, never was there such a heavy burden.
Joseph:	Mary, listen to this holy man. What prophecies he is pronouncing! He is announcing marvels concerning Jesus which must not be forgotten.

Our Lady:	It is certainly something to marvel at; I keep all these things in my heart.
Simeon:	May you two be blessed by the right hand of God the Father. I proclaim you very fortunate, for it appears clearly that God loves you, as he has committed such a treasure into your care, my friends. May God grant that you guard him well! And thou, lady, look upon thy Son whom thou holdest as the dearest of thy possessions. Behold, this Child is set for the fall and rising again of many in Israel; and for a sign which shall be spoken against; (Yea, a sword shall pierce through thy own soul also,) that the thoughts of many hearts may be revealed.[8]
Anna, the Prophetess:	
	True God, true Lord of our law, I confess all my sins to thee. I am unworthy to see such a divine Person, very holy, very high Mediator, as the sovereign Redeemer whom I perceive in my presence. Christ beloved by the prophets, well art thou found among us, very benign, desired flower! May the power of God be praised for thy divine descent! Rejoice greatly, all good people of Jerusalem, Zion, and Bethlehem; make great and small festivities. Here is your Saviour: your deliverance is near!
Joseph:	Lady, now you are purified as the law commands. Since we have made our offering, we mut return home without delay to the city of Nazareth where our home is.
Our Lady:	May God guide us by his grace!

Here they go away into their first places.   (G)   Then they go swiftly to Nazareth and Simeon returns to his place.   (M)

Scene 39. The Court of King Herod

Herod:	We do not at all understand the manners, the reasons, or the true motives of those Kings, who departed from our presence a long time ago, and who have not returned this way as they promised.

8. Luke 2:29–35.

Hermogenes:	Sire, I suspect they were deceived by their vision. Their star and story were only an illusion because of which, I believe, they were ashamed to return.
Herod:	Hermogenes, you speak well. They have really been ashamed, for which reason we are happy and joyful, for this matter has amounted to nothing. As for the Christ and his coming, we will never believe a word of it.
Arphazac:	Those Kings held frivolous opinions, sire. Never think of them.

Here warn Zorobabel and Gamaliel to go grandly to Herod's Palace. (M)

Gamaliel:	True master of justice and law, may God guard you and your assembly of lords!
Herod:	Gamaliel of noble birth, may you be welcome among us! What has happened recently? You seem all distraught.
Gamaliel:	Sire, here is the situation: we do not know whether you remember the Three Kings who passed by here, and whether you remember the birth of the Christ that they announced to you, and whether you remember the star that signified that the Christ is born and has come to earth in the flesh.
Herod:	We have a very good memory of that, for the Kings lied to us about their return. But as for this birth, we have never given it a thought since then, for fear that we might be caught up in some mad fantasy.
Gamaliel:	Lord King, I certify to you that the news is revealed throughout all the land of Judaea that the King they were seeking is born, just as they were saying, but nobody knows the place.
Herod:	What are you saying?
Zorobabel:	It is as he reports. As for this mystery, some have seen it who affirm having held the little Babe in their arms.
Herod:	But are they truly reputable persons who sow such rumors?

Roboan:	The sanest, the wisest, the most praiseworthy persons in the city of Jerusalem say that the mystery has taken place.
Herod:	Here is new devilry! Here is aggravation of grief and contradiction to our wishes! My heart overflows with wrath. Ha! False accursed line of traitorous Arabian Kings, you have wished to defraud us by false and treacherous means, and you have known how to guard against returning this way to us!
Adracus:	Sire, cease your wrath!

Scene 40. The Flight into Egypt

God the Father:	Gabriel, go warn Joseph, our devoted caretaker, to take the Virgin Mary with her mild Infant Jesus, and to go away without tarrying any longer to dwell in the land of Egypt. And let him dwell and inhabit there until a time that will be indicated to him.
Gabriel:	Father of Heaven, your command will be accomplished; I am going there directly.

Here remind Gabriel to approach Joseph in Nazareth. (M)

Gabriel:	Joseph, hear my voice: Arise, and take the young Child and his mother, and flee into Egypt, and be thou there until I bring thee word: for Herod will seek the young Child to destroy him.9
Joseph:	We must no longer stay here. Mary, arise quickly! We must flee into Egypt for a while. The Angel has told me that we must do this to avert a great misfortune.
Our Lady:	The night is very dark and murky; let us go away by a secret route.

Here Our Lady mounts on the donkey with the Child, and they go away into Egypt. (G) Then they go away with their donkey. (M)

9. Matthew 2:13.

Scene 41. The Second Diablerie

***Remind Satan to be outside Hell to speak on cue. Prepare some
great noise to be made on cue in Hell.   (M)***

Satan:	Every day I search for means and ruses by which to succeed in my mischief, but I cannot find any means by which to gain anything, even when I use the most spiteful tricks. Of what use to me is this Mary who has given birth to I do not know what Son, because of whom people are holding such solemn festivities? The conception was hidden from me and the birth was entirely hidden, so that I knew nothing. I greatly fear that I have been deceived, and that there is something in the wind that will afterward cause me great mourning. There is no way for me to know without burrowing down into Hell to ask Lucifer for counsel and remedy. Help, Devils! Come in troups, in masses, with great puffs of smoke from the eternal flaming sulfur. Come quickly to help me!
Lucifer:	Arise, Devils! Run to Satan, our ambassador. He is shrieking so loudly that he must have seen a very hideous sight, or he may have been ambushed.
Beelzebub:	I will leap into the fray to find out what plot is hatching.

The Devils come out of Hell.   (M)

Cerberus:	How art thou, Satan? Art thou enraged or mad? What dost thou need? What hast thou found? Who has dragged thee back here?
Astaroth:	Let blows thicker than peas in a pot fall on this pilgrim!

***Then let Satan be very well beaten and make a great tempest
in Hell.   (M)***

Lucifer:	Stop! Do not touch him, Astaroth: I forbid thee to touch him or I'll have thee bound. Satan, cast thy glance, deadlier than a

The Valenciennes Hellmouth

	basilisk, over this way. In horrible speech laced with deadly words, tell us how thou hast accomplished thy task.
Satan:	If I must tell, let no soul hit my face; I am half out of my wits. Lucifer, according to what I sense, our brigade will soon have the luck to have very foul company.
Beelzebub:	How? Why? Thou dost not tell us anything worthwhile.
Lucifer:	Let him speak, you ribald Devils; let no soul hinder him.
Satan:	King of Hell, I tell thee that in the land of Galilee is I do not know what woman named Mary. She is a rather young Virgin, the most courteous, the most beautiful, the sweetest, the kindliest, the most virtuous, and the worthiest person who lives among the pure in heart today. I have watched her and I have tried to entrap her by any malicious trick, but there is no evil sin or vice by which I can possess her soul.
Lucifer:	How can that be? Dost thou not know how to deceive her? Thou, disloyal Satan, who art so subtle and treacherous?
Satan:	Nothing deceives her. Her life is a marvel; her soul belongs entirely to God. When I so much as look at her, I feel as if I were burning, blazing on a pyre of a hundred thousand logs. Then I go away all bewildered, howling like a mad wolf.
Lucifer:	Ah, false condemned serpent, beware what thy tongue proposes!
Satan:	She is the holiest person whom any tongue could describe. I saw Judith, I saw Esther, I saw Rachel, I saw Leah. There is no comparison; this one surpasses them all.
Cerberus:	Satan, thou dost plunge us into great uncertainty and discomfort.
Satan:	Yet I will tell you worse news: this Virgin has had a Child. I have not been able to find out how or when, but I am certain that she has never been touched by any man. Yet she has had a handsome Son, by whom we will all be discomfited, for the rumor is now flying that he is the Christ, coming to redeem all humanity. I saw him presented at the Temple, and I heard it

	publicly stated that he is the authentic Saviour who must deliver the Jews.
Lucifer:	False dragon! False famished mastiff! Perverse venimous tortoise! Dost thou bear me this news? Well, sire, does Herod know anything about this Child?
Satan:	Yes, he has been informed of it by the Three Kings from far-away lands. I did insinuate one idea into Herod's thoughts: that all the tiny infants in Bethlehem and Judaea should be slaughtered, so that among them One might be found who is called the King of the Jews.
Lucifer:	Oh, what a noble sort of counsel! In all our Hell there is no other Devil who could have dreamed of such counsel. Now arise, Satan, and go finish this matter. Bring Herod's soul back with you.
Satan:	Let Astaroth take a turn and go; let him perform the rest.
Lucifer:	Thou shalt go thyself; stop chattering. Thou dost thyself harm to rebel.
Satan:	At least make Berich bear me company.
Lucifer:	All of you go! May the horrible family of the damned guide and lead you, and bring you back to such torments that you all burn in eternal sulfur in the depths of the infernal pit!

Here they go away toward Herod.   (G)   Remind Joseph to speak after the tempest is made.   (M)

Scene 42. The Fall of the Idols

Joseph:	May God be thanked, for we have traveled quite swiftly and we have arrived in Egypt without any danger.

Here be ready to make the idols of the Temple fall on cue.   (M)

Our Lady:	Sire, let us think about lodging in this nearby city, for we have experienced labor and weariness; we need to rest a little.

Joseph: Dear lady, I obey your wishes, and I pity you more than I can say. Follow me; I am going ahead.

Here they go away to take lodgings, and nearby there must be a Temple where there are several idols, which will tumble down at their coming. (G)   Then Joseph and Mary must pass into Egypt with Mary holding Jesus in her arms, in front of a Temple and, as soon as she passes by, the idols must fall to the ground. (M)[10]

Theodas, First Priest of the idols of Egypt:
              The sun has risen on a clear day and fine morning. It is appropriate that on this day we sacrifice to our great gods; let us go there soon.

Torquatus, Second Priest:
              That is wise. There will be no god or goddess who does not receive abundant sacrifice, each according to rank. Mohammed will be the first, then Apollo, Venus, and Mercury.

Theodas: Let us walk swiftly to the Temple so that we may pay homage to our gods.

Then the priests go to the Temple. Organ music or other music while they approach. (M)

Torquatus, being at the Temple:
              What is this? Here is an act of arrogance to which I am not accustomed: here are all our great gods, fallen upside down!

Theodas: I have looked carefully above and below, but I have not found any image that is not lying on the paving stones. I do not know who cast them down thus. See here the great god Mohammed, who has his head broken in pieces. See here Venus, all broken. See here Apollo and Jupiter. See Saturn and Adonis.

Torquatus: Who has done such battle with them that they have toppled two by two? Has there come One stronger than they, or has

10. The Fall of the Idols appears in the Apocrypha in I Infancy of Jesus Christ and in the Gospel of Pseudo-Matthew. See also Isaiah, 19:1.

	some God come into this land, who has waged such great war with them as to make them suffer such reverses?
Theodas:	We will have to assemble the priests and discuss the matter.
Torquatus:	That is the right procedure so that we may know the cause.

Then they return to their places. *(M)*

Scene 43. The Decree of King Herod

Herod:	You know that not long ago, we received warning of an Infant born in this country who is proclaimed King of the Jews. This is detrimental to our interests. We must employ the rigor of justice to put down such an erroneous claim.
Adracus:	Lord King, your commands will be obeyed without refusal.
Herod:	Here is our intention: to put to harsh and cruel death all male children in Bethlehem and Judaea so that this hapless King, if he is born, dies with the rest without being a pretender to our crown.
Arphazac:	The decree is fine and good; it is proper to execute it.
Herod:	Hermogenes, you must count the time since the star first appeared, for several persons say that the Child was born on the day when it appeared.
Hermogenes:	Those who study the story carefully say expressly that it was two years ago, or nearly two years ago; the second year has already begun.
Herod:	That is accurate enough counting. To make the execution order conform to that counting, it is decreed to kill all male children under two years of age, equally, without excepting anyone. Arise, soldiers of the guard! Show us a little what you are worth. Go away into Bethlehem and put to death all male children under two years of age that you find there. If any executioner is so foolhardy as to spare sister or brother, or to take pity on father or mother, or to be corrupted by bribes, be assured that his best fate will be to hang on the gallows without trial. Now go quickly.

Here Adracus remains with the King, and all the other men go away. (G) Then they go away, but Adracus remains with Herod. Remember to warn the wet nurses to be ready. (M)

Scene 44. The Massacre of the Innocents

Arphazac: Forward! Step lightly to the task, companions. See Agripart here, who is afraid. He says that fathers do not bother him, but he greatly fears mothers, who often have great courage.

Agripart: We will not have a face left that will not be destroyed by claws.

Hermogenes: Come, come, companions! We must work on that matron. See there? An infant, just such as we must kill.

Agripart: I would like to prove my sword. Woman, give me this babe, if you don't mind.

Rap, Wet Nurse: My friend, what do you want to do with my babe when you hold him?

Agripart: Don't be upset; you will see. I'm only doing it for fun.

Rap: You may hold him. See the handsome and tender babe? Please take him very gently. Soon you will make his heart fail!

Here he kills him. (G)

Hermogenes: Take him; carry him away to boil, or make a fat pastry out of him.

Rap: Ah! False murderers, are you such? False thieves, false perverse tyrants, have you come here for such a wicked and ugly purpose? Alas! My sweet little babe. Alas! My very gentle newborn. Alas! Now thy life is taken from thee. Alas! Now I cannot have thee back. Never shall I know joy again until my death.

Arphazac: There, woman, without any moans: is that your little babe that you are carrying?

Rachel, Wet Nurse:

> Do not doubt it at all. He is mine; such I believe him to be.

Arphazac: How old is he?

Rachel: Thirteen months. He is hardly any older.

Agripart: Arphazac, that's all you need. Handle him a bit and see how much he weighs.

Arphazac: Willingly. There, woman, give him to me. He must pass into my hands.

Rachel: My friends and human brothers, alas! Do you want to injure this poor creature, this poor innocent babe?

Arphazac: Now ask him if he feels it.

Here he kills him. **(G)**

Arphazac: Take him and go roast him, woman. I have given him medicine from which he will never recover.

Agripart: Come, gallants, let us turn our brigade that way toward the other soldiers. Faster!

Rachel: Ah! False dogs and tyrant villains. Ah! Hearts of disloyal murderers, infamous men, wicked slaughterers of a sweet and tender child who has never done you any harm, I pray to God who made all that you will die a harsh death!

Andrometa, Wet Nurse:

> Arbeline, may the great God of Israel guard you! Let us save our babes somewhere. They are putting all male infants under two years of age to death.

Arbeline, Wet Nurse:

> What horror! Alas! Good neighbor, where does this evil decree come from, and who makes them do it? I do not know where we can hide.

Andrometa: Herod, the evil King, has issued this decree. May God curse him and finish his days in misery!

Arbeline: What wilt thou do, sorrowing mother? Where wilt thou best hide thy babe? Must you see thine infant die cruelly before thine eyes? Alas! My son, my only care, here is a pitiful destiny! Accursed be the day that ever I conceived thee in my womb, if thou must fall into the hands of thy persecutors!

Andreometa: Ah, son, for thee I feel such sorrow!

Agripart: Do you wish to oppose the law and the King's command?

Arbeline: What will you do, wicked tyrant? Let the poor innocent live.

Agripart: If I do not soon have a rescuer—

Arbeline: What will you do, wicked tyrant?

Agripart: This bitch is pulling my arm so hard that I am afraid she will kill me!

Andrometa: What will you do, wicked tyrant? Let the poor innocent live.

Hermogenes: Do I not know the lesson without a book? Am I not a fine archer?

Andrometa: Truly, or a clever butcher! As for that, you know enough.

Hermogenes: Go to the others; these are dead. We have that many less to destroy.

Arbeline: Oh true God, who could describe the great distress that I feel? My mind and wits are forsaking me.

Andrometa: Be comforted, Arbeline. Whoever wishes to consider our estate will see that my mourning is not less than yours, but still, it must be moderated.

Arbeline: Oh poor heart of weary mother, drowned in depths of tears, heart broken by agony and sorrow! I can no longer live, nor great distress endure, my son, whose death crushes me.

Scene 45. The Death of King Herod's Son

Medusa, Wet Nurse of Herod's Son:
     Sabine?

Sabine, his Chambermaid:
     What do you please, mistress? I was playing a little.

Medusa: Make ready the infant chariot for my lord Herod's son. He is growing up rapidly and he needs to go out into the fields.

Massacre of the Innocents and Death of King Herod

Sabine:	My mistress, I have thought of it; here you see the chariot prepared. Sire, you have been indoors too long; you must play outside a little.

Then Sabine takes the chariot and puts the wooden doll inside. *(M)*

Medusa:	Now take him outdoors wherever you please, and be careful that he comes to no harm.
Sabine:	I will take proper care of him. Just leave him to me and believe that he will be well tended.
Hermogenes:	In a short time we have finished our business with this riffraff.
Arphazac:	I killed babes more numerous than pieces of straw. I have dispatched more than two thousand babes in a month.
Agripart:	And I, three thousand. Truly, I think, four thousand.
Hermogenes:	You men are braggarts, but what else? That is all your skill.
Agripart:	Why, sire?
Hermogenes:	Can't you see? See a babe over there who is being promenaded.
Agripart:	He will suffer a bloody evil fate if I can reach him swiftly. Now look what a trick my hand performs, Arphazac.
Arphazac:	Bah! You put too much into it.
Agripart:	There he is, suddenly sliced in two. Is that not well done?
Medusa:	Ah! False murderers, what have you done? You have evilly murdered Herod's own son! What horror has come to pass!
Agripart:	If only he had not come so near!
Medusa:	Very soon I will make you bray loudly.

Scene 46. The Death of King Herod

Then she goes to King Herod. *(M)*

Medusa:	Lord King, a very great misfortune has just occurred, and the deed is so criminal that I hardly dare name it.
Herod:	How is my son doing?
Medusa:	Badly. Your dear son whom you placed in my care has been killed. None of the several servants could protect him.
Herod:	Who has done this?
Medusa:	Your own soldiers killed him along with the other infants.
Adracus:	Sire, I have been informed that the soldiers did not recognize him at all.
Herod:	Ah! Fortune, false enemy! Fortune, disguised beast who knows how to do all evil! These are the tricks that thou dost know how to play. Thou dost expect my mourning to alter me, but even this raging grief will not diminish my courage for the persecution and terrible slaughter that I began.
Medusa:	Sire, since I am released from further duties, I take my leave now.

Then she goes away. *(M)*

Hermogenes:	Let us go immediately to the royal palace, for the King's special decree has been thoroughly executed.
Arphazac:	I know neither city nor town surrounding Bethlehem that has not wept at our coming. Never was there such sorrow.
Hermogenes:	Dreaded Lord King, your decree has been accomplished. The populace has been saddened since we left here.
Herod:	Have you done as we said? Is there no remaining infant?
Agripart:	All are dead.
Herod:	You have labored well. Is there no remaining infant under the age of two years who has not been thrown out the window?
Agripart:	All are slaughtered.
Herod:	That was masterfully spoken; we rejoice in your exploits and in their results. One sole point causes remorse, concerning our infant son who died by error, due to our own negligence. We

	do not blame you for this. We wish to bear our grief patiently as long as we are convinced that this Christ, our adversary, is harmed, killed, and destroyed by our decree.
Adracus:	We must say that it is so, for since all the male infants have suffered such evil fates, that they are dead, I say that he has not escaped unless he has recourse to magic.

Here warn Satan and Astaroth to be around Herod. *(M)*

Herod:	Lords in whom our hope of abundant health lies, we feel very strongly attacked by various maladies, the harshest and most perverse maladies that ever a creature's body has suffered.
Arphazac:	What causes these maladies? Sire, have you suffered for a long time?
Herod:	Arphazac, the maladies began as soon as we put our three sons to death, when we promptly discovered their plot to overthrow us. Then we heard that our fourth son was killed in infancy, which greatly increased our sorrow.
Hermogenes:	Do not make your maladies worse by becoming enraged, Lord King. Three sons remain, bold princes of great fame, to succeed to the kingdom that you hold in peace.
Herod:	You speak truly, Hermogenes, but the two sons who have always opposed us will not come to power after us. We will give the kingdom to our youngest son, truly, but on the condition that he must never be presumptuously crowned by any man other than the Emperor of Rome, our sovereign lord. Alas! Lords, great misery and harsh, intolerable torment overwhelm us, and neither God nor Devil lets us rest!
Arphazac:	Lie down.
Satan:	That is well spoken. I do not know who will put him to bed, but never will he arise; I'll wager my hooded cape.
Astaroth:	Satan, be careful that this false oppressor of innocents does not escape.

Herod:	Alas! What distress I feel! Help! What unbearable torments! I see more than a hundred thousand Devils, the most hideous imaginable, who are waiting to carry me away.
Salome, Herod's Sister:	
	My brother, be courageous and take heart.
Herod:	Ah, Salome, dear sister! I am living, and yet death is before me. I am dying, and yet I am still alive. I am mad, and yet I am quite sane. No man was ever so punished.
Adracus:	Do not approach so near to him, lady, because of the foul smell. He stinks most horribly because his flesh is corrupted; the worms are eating him alive and coming out of his orifices.
Herod:	I realize that the Jews will hold a great celebration at my death. Therefore, sister, I command you to have all the Jewish nobles of high rank in our prisons slaughtered upon my tombstone, after my soul has departed. Thus you will be able to force the Jews to lament my death and to solemnize my passing.
Salome:	My brother, I will not fail, although your command is harsh and proud. It will be accomplished; make good cheer and rejoice.
Herod:	Now give us an apple and a knife with which to peel it.
Salome:	You shall have it; you see it is ready.

She gives him an apple and a knife. (M)

Herod:	Alas! My feet! Alas! My head! Spite and furious rage! I can bear no more without going mad; such is my distress.

Remember to warn those in Hell to prepare their things to welcome Herod's soul, on cue. (M)

Satan:	Wicked, prideful man, plunge this knife into thy bowels without trying to endure any more.

Herod:	Devils, I can endure no more. I must obey you all. Ah! Death, hurry, false bitch; this I do to advance thee. With my heart, body, and mind, I commend myself to all the Devils!

Here Herod kills himself with a knife.   (G)   Then Herod stabs himself with a knife in the belly.   (M)

Scene 47. The Third Diablerie

Satan:	Come! Let us two nimbly remove this false, despairing murderer's soul.
Astaroth:	His lodging is already prepared; let us carry him straight into Hell.

Then the Devils take Herod's soul, and not his body, and carry it away into Hell.   (M)

Satan:	Lucifer, see what prey we are bringing to our assembly.
Astaroth:	It's your minister, Herod, who is searching for his new home.
Lucifer:	He comes from afar; we must celebrate his arrival properly. For his salvation, christen him in boiling lead and burning metals. He has his reward according to our laws.

Here the Devils make a tempest.   (G)   Then let a terrible noise be made in Hell for Herod.   (M)

Scene 48. The Court of King Herod

Adracus:	Never did the body of any creature endure such a dreadful death.
Hermogenes:	My sense of justice tells me that divine punishment has brought him down with such force.
Arphazac:	There is nothing left to do but bury him and perform the solemnities that are his due.

Salome:	Do not doubt that my heart is broken with grief to see my brother in this condition, but I cannot improve it.

Music. (G)

Scene 49. The Howeward Journey of the Holy Family

God the Father:	According to the seasons that we have ordained for our Son Jesus to reign, it is time for him to return from Egypt, where he dwells with his mother. Gabriel, go announce to Joseph that he should think of returning to Israel.
Gabriel:	Father, I will do it lovingly.

Music. (G) *Then Gabriel goes. (M)*

Gabriel:	Joseph, my friend! Arise, and take the young Child and his mother, and go into the land of Israel: for they are dead which sought the young Child's life.[11]
Joseph:	Mary, it pleases our Lord God that we return to our native country.
Our Lady:	Sire, since we know the will of God, let us keep his virtuous counsel.
Joseph:	Now may all-perfect God guide us on our homeward journey.

Here Joseph returns, Our Lady on her donkey with the Infant as before. (G) Then Joseph brings back Our Lady and the Infant on her donkey, as he had led the donkey away, and he leads it back to his House in Nazareth. (M)

---

11. Matthew 2:20.

Scene 50. Epilogue

The Actor: Lords, who have seen the performance of the Nativity of our Saviour Jesus Christ, if we have said, written, done, or performed anything incorrectly, may you pardon us for the love of God. We wish to hold to the true path without error. We charge each of you to keep the path of true faith in your heart. Now to finish our mystery joyfully and honorably, let us all thank God the Father by singing *Te Deum laudamus!*

SHELLEY SEWALL is a theater historian specializing in the French medieval religious theater. She holds a master of letters in French medieval studies from the University of St. Andrews. She has also completed a master of arts in drama and theater from the University of Hawaii, a bachelor of arts in French from the University of California, Berkeley, postgraduate courses in French literature at Harvard University, and a teaching diploma from the University of Geneva. She is currently teaching French at the University of California, Davis, and is working on an iconographic study of the miniatures in the Arras *Passion*.